# FIVERR STAR

## How to make 2000$ a month on Fiverr

## Working 2 hours a day from home

### A book
### By:

Gianluca Sidoti

# Legal Notice:

# CONTENTS

# CHAPTER. 1

## INTRODUCTION

Thank you for purchasing my ebook. My name is Gianluca and I've been on Fiverr since mid 2013. Since then, I've used my knowledge of internet marketing, business and sales to create an amazing second income using Fiverr. I currently make $4000 a month, with only approximately 8 hours of work a week and I am one of the Top Rated Sellers on Fiverr.

My success didn't start right away; it took a lot of experimenting and trial and error. In this book, I will save you the months of headaches and wasted money to get you started in earning a great second income (or even a great full-time income from home). Yes, making enough money to quit your job is possible on Fiverr. It's not a scheme or a scam, and it's not a trick, it is just the truth. Just check out Fiverr's blog if you don't believe me. Every month they feature their top sellers with an article detailing their success stories.

Can I promise you that kind of income? Of course not.

Fiverr is just a vehicle for you to generate some money. It all depends on who you are, how you work and how lucky you are. There potential to make some kind of income is definitely there no matter who you are, you just need to apply yourself and apply some of what you learn in this book.

Do the success stories you read on Fiverr show you how to replicate that success? Of course not. This book will lay out a blueprint—scratch that, this book will HOLD YOUR HAND and will give you a formula so that you can make upwards of what I make on Fiverr and perhaps even more depending on what twists you put on my ideas or how creative you are.

## "YOU MAKE WHAT ON FIVERR?? PROVE IT!"

Sales Analytics

| $4,040 | 7,308 | $8 | 99% |
|---|---|---|---|
| EARNED THIS MONTH | ORDERS CREATED | AVG. SELLING PRICE | POSITIVE RATING |
| NEW ORDERS | GIG EXTRA ORDERS | MULTIPLE ORDERS | DELIVERED ORDERS |

Here you can see proof that I've earned just over $4000 in March 2017 on Fiverr. I am not selling any fancy gigs that require a talent or skill not many people have or gigs that require a lot of work. I am selling gigs that are in high demand and can easily be done by almost anyone, which I will go into in this ebook.

## WHY MAKE THIS BOOK? WHY GIVE THIS AWAY IF YOU'RE SO SUCCESSFUL?

Truth be told, I did of course see earning potential in sharing my knowledge and formula to others so they can make money on Fiverr. But also, sharing this formula with you does not hurt my future Fiverr earnings. Fiverr, at the time this book was first written (April 2017), was the 132th most visited website in the world and the 69th in the United States. Fiverr is only poised to grow even larger and has been growing at an exponential rate over the past 2 years. Sharing this knowledge with you won't saturate the Fiverr market. So picking up this ebook a few months later, after many people have already read and copied my formula, won't hurt you since there's room for everyone. Not to mention, even if you don't sell the gigs I recommend selling, I still offer solid tips and advice to optimize your sales no matter what you decide to sell on Fiverr.

## HOW TO GET THE MOST OUT OF THIS BOOK

If you want to get the most out of this book, I highly suggest you follow along as you read. I try to include screenshots when I can, but it's easier to absorb the information when you read and do it at the same time.

After I first released this book back in 2017, I launched a forum for Fiverr sellers to come together and exchange reviews and tips.

Also, while it's tempting to flip ahead to the meat of the book, I suggest reading this book from beginning to end and in order. I will often refer to tips from previous chapters. Also, it's important to not miss any information. There are a lot of little things or little details in this book.

Every single one of them, when implemented in entirety, will really help you be successful on Fiverr.

## UNDERSTANDING THE 80/20 PRINCIPLE

Throughout this ebook, I will refer to the 80/20 principle or the "Pareto principle". It means, generally, that 80% of the effects come from 20% of the causes. You can apply this to anything but it is most commonly applied in business. I'm a big believer in this rule and follow it for all my ventures, startups and projects whether they're financially motivated or not. I even applied it when I wrote this book. It's important to understand and learn this rule. I learned to apply this to Fiverr realizing 80% of my sales came from 20% of my gigs. I could bore you with it in this e-book but there are a lot of free resources out there, including Wikipedia, which can do a good job of explaining it to you.

It's not crucial to your success on Fiverr nor will I try to push my business theories and beliefs on you. It's just a small detail I thought it would be worth sharing, especially if it ended up helping you on Fiverr!

## THE CULTURE OF FIVERR

Fiverr isn't a site like Ebay, Craigslist, Upwork or anything else. Yeah, I know it's a $5 marketplace and that is Fiverr's gimmick. But let me get into a theory of mine really quickly. I think Fiverr has invented a new kind of website and marketplace. I think it's a trend that will really grow and we will start to see many more sites like this, perhaps even see a site like Upwork go this way. Fiverr is what I like to call a "social marketplace". It's more personal and community-like than say a site like Ebay or even Upwork. People put their faces on their gigs. Their brand is themselves.

Why's this important or why should you care? Well, I dive into this a bit in my ebook but if you treat Fiverr like just a marketplace or another freelancing website, you may not fulfill your true earning potential. You can't be faceless on Fiverr; you need a little bit of personality. This is not going to make or break your success on Fiverr but Fiverr does have its' own unique style and culture. It is just something important to consider.

## HOW TO MAKE MONEY ON FIVERR

Fiverr takes a good chunk out of all the money you make. At first, $1of your $5 gig may not seem like much, but when you start to make $1000 a month or more, that 20% Fiverr takes becomes more apparent.

This puts people off to the website. They start to think "why would I do all this work for a measly $4?" But of course that's the wrong approach.

There are people making a killing on Fiverr right now. If you thought I was making a lot of money on Fiverr, I make peanuts compared to some of the biggest sellers on Fiverr.

When we look at a Fiverr seller like Ozzieuk, who sells SEO services on Fiverr, we can clearly see how many deliveries this user completes per day.

RECENT DELIVERIES

Taking a look at this screenshot (an old screenshot before Fiverr changed seller profiles and his this information), we see that the highlighted peak is 150 deliveries. A rough estimate for the amount of deliveries Ozzieuk completes per day would be 100.

100 deliveries per day would mean roughly an average of more than 100 orders per day, factoring in the orders that likely get cancelled.

Now, for the sake of simplicity, we are not going to factor in gig extra orders or gig multiple orders for now.

If we say Ozzieuk delivers 100 orders a day, 100 orders x $4 per order = $400 per day.

Multiply that by 365 days in a year and Top Rated Seller Ozzieuk makes a whopping $146,000 per year on Fiverr. The crazy part? (as if making over 100k on Fiverr per year wasn't crazy enough) This is the conservative estimate!

Like I said, I didn't factor in the gig extras and gig multiples, of which Ozzieuk charges and sells A LOT, which would put his yearly earnings on Fiverr closer to something like $300,000-$500,000 USD per year!

Now, I'm not exactly sure how the income taxing system works over there in the country of Uk where Ozzieuk resides but I do know that that is still an amazing salary even after taxes.

Granted, it is very likely Ozzieuk has expenses. He pays for software, proxies, lists, and maybe even outsourcing and those expenses add up but even if the net income at the end of the year was $100,000, it would still be an amazing feat.

There are two ways to make money on Fiverr.

The first way is by volume. 1 order that earns you $4 is nothing.

However, 30-40 orders per day? That's going to make you $120-$160 per day.

Volume however, is the most difficult way to make money on Fiverr. It requires you to be picked up frequently in searches. If your gigs don't have more than 10k impressions in the last 30 days, it will be very hard for you to have this kind of volume.

You need to sell in-demand gigs and configure your gigs so that they are picked up for frequent and high volume search terms.

Ozzieuk has 30 gigs. He is able to have this number of gigs

because he is a Top Rated Seller. However, as a level 2 Fiverr seller, you are able to have 20. 20 is still a really good number and if you want to improve your chances of getting picked up in more searches and potentially receive more orders per day, then you will want to always have a full 20 gigs. If you're level 1, always have 15 active gigs, if you're new, always have 7 active gigs.

The second way to make money on Fiverr is to increase the average selling price of your gigs.

You do this by including gig extras on all of your gigs and by encouraging people to buy gig multiples and gig extras. Alternatively, you can simply charge more using Gig Packages, a new feature that Fiverr has introduced.

How do you do this?

The easiest way is to create a gig where the essentials are in the gig extras or gig packages, or it is essential to purchase gig extras.

**Let me explain.**

If I were to have a voiceover gig, I would offer something like $5 for 50 words. Most people, on average, require a lot more than that when they require a voiceover for a video. This is encouraging them to buy multiples or choose a more expensive gig package. If they want 400 words, they're going to have to pony up and spend $40, of which I would earn $32.

Now, to put that in perspective, to earn that much in volume, I would have to receive 8 orders. It's a lot easier to sell 1 gig for $40 than to sell a gig 8 times in a day for $40 on Fiverr.

Another thing is to put essential or expensive packaged services in the gig extras or more expensive gig packages. If you look at the gig extras for Ozzieuk, you'll see he has gig extra packages for $100. So much for selling a $5 service on Fiverr, huh?

All of his gig extras for all his gigs are like this.

They are packages and often times, he puts a lot of value in his gig extras (think 2 for 1 kind of deals) which encourages buyers to purchase his gig extras and thus, increasing his average selling price.

Ozzieuk is fortunate enough that he gets the best of both worlds. He gets a massive volume of sales on Fiverr and he also sells a lot of gig extras.

The good news is, you only need one or the other to make money on Fiverr.

If you want more perspective on how order volume and gig extras can drastically change your income, I suggest you check out the Fiverr Calculator.

# CHAPTER 2:

## YOUR FIVERR ACCOUNT

**ACCOUNT CREATION**

If you don't already have a Fiverr account, go ahead and make one now before continuing on through this e-book. You will also need a PayPal account to withdraw your money that you've earned through Fiverr. To create a new account, go to Fiverr.com and click on "Join" in the upper- right hand corner.

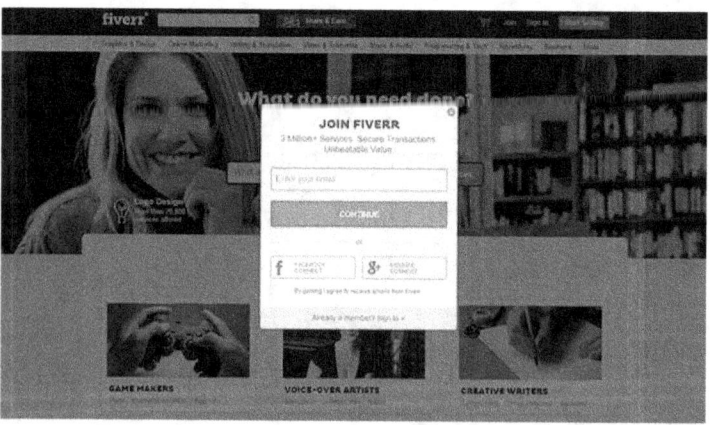

Here, you can join with Facebook if you wish but I'd rather you make an account from scratch. When choosing a username, it is helpful to pick a relevant username. For example, if you will be doing SEO and backlink gigs, something like "SEO_Guy" or "SEOking" would both be good choices.

It's important to do this since you are branding yourself. Fiverr users see your username and they will recognize you are specializing in that type of gig. This will also encourage users to click on your profile to view other gigs you offer since they will assume you only offer gigs of this type.

After registering, confirm your email by clicking the link in the email Fiverr will send you to the email you signed up with.

## ACCOUNT SETUP

**Profile Photo:** If you are confident having your face on the internet, I highly recommend you upload a picture of yourself as a profile photo.

Fiverr is a very social marketplace. You will see many people sit in front of a camera and describe their gig. If you upload a picture of yourself in your profile, you will seem more trusting and you will get more orders because of this.

If you do not want to use a photo of yourself, you can also decide to upload a picture of an attractive girl. Why? I will get into this in detail later in the ebook, but women seem to get more sales on Fiverr than men. An attractive girl in your profile will also attract more clicks to your profile, thus allowing more people to see all the gigs you offer. Trust me on this. I've experimented with male profiles vs. female profiles when I made multiple Fiverr accounts. The female accounts ALWAYS have more sales.

**Something About You:** This section is pretty important. It appears in the right sidebar of every one of your gig's pages as well as on your profile. Here you should describe yourself briefly and give some background on your expertise. **At the end of your bio I highly recommend a call to action**. "Check out my other gigs on my profile for more SEO for only $5!" would be a good call to action at the bottom of your bio. This is important because on every page of your gigs, Fiverr users will see this call to action and encourage them to see your other gigs when most of them wouldn't have otherwise.

**I Can Communicate In:** If you are capable of typing/reading in other languages, this is very worthwhile. Right now, there are a few language options on Fiverr which can help you get a few more sales a month since not everyone who comes to Fiverr speaks or read English.

**Your Story in One Line:** Here's where you can share your expertise in one line. What best sums up what you do in one sentence? Here's an example of one: "Internet Marketing PRO, SEO Expert, Traffic Guru"

## FIVERR LEVELS

If you haven't made your Fiverr account already it's really important you do right now. This is because Fiverr has seller levels which partly depend on the age of your account. I will go into further detail explaining what these levels are, what they do and why they're important.

Seller levels are important since they place a badge or icon next to your name which gives you credibility to other users. Besides that, seller levels open up new options for you as a seller.

## NEW SELLER

Benefits: 7 active gigs, 2 gig extras ($5, $10, $20), 5 gig multiples, send custom offers up to $325

## LEVEL 1

Requirements: 30 days member and completed at least 10 orders with excellent ratings.

Benefits: 15 active gigs, 4 gig extras ($5, $10, $20, $30), 10 gig multiples, send custom offers up to $1,500

## LEVEL 2

Requirements: 60 days member and completed at least 50 orders with excellent ratings.

Benefits: 20 active gigs, 5 gig extras ($5, $10, $20, $40, $50), 15 gig multiples, send custom offers

## TOP RATED SELLER

Requirements: Top Rated sellers are manually chosen. You need to have a high sales volume, seniority, very high rating across all of your gigs, and good customer service. This is very difficult to achieve but with this ebook it is possible. Don't fret though: your goal should be to at least achieve Level

2. This badge will help increase your sales volume.

Benefits: 30 active gigs, 6 gig extras ($5, $10, $20, $40, $50, $100), 20 gig multiples, send custom offers

# Chapter 3:

# Creating A New Gig And Setting It Up For Maximum Earnings

I'm now going to go into how I create a gig that will be picked up in the searches. This section will be very general. When I go on to talk about what to sell on Fiverr in the next chapter, I will go into detail as to what to put exactly for each type of gig I suggest. I will cover exactly what keywords, titles, images, categories and more. For now let's look at how I create a gig and then what my "secret sauce" is.

Let's create a gig. At the top right of Fiverr.com, you will see Start Selling or Sales, depending on whether you just created your account or not. Under "My Sales" click on "Create A Gig".

## GIG TITLE

The first thing Fiverr will ask for is your gig title. Fiverr limits all gig titles to 80 characters max but do not actually create a gig using the full 80 characters in your title. The most characters you should use are around 50 characters. The **ideal gig title length is 16-50 characters**. Why? Long gig titles do not rank as well in Fiverr's searches as shorter titles do. But obviously you don't want to force your gig title to be too short either. Try to make your gig title as long as possible until it is at 50 characters. Using as many keywords as possible in the title will help it be picked up in Fiverr searches. An example of a good gig title:

I will get you 1000 real looking Twitter followers

This title contains 3 keywords that people frequently search: real, Twitter, followers. Even though in this case the Twitter followers being sold aren't real, this gig will still show in a search "real Twitter followers".

## CATEGORY

This is very important. Having your gig in the best category and sub- category possible will mean more clicks and conversions when users are browsing categories just checking to see what kinds of gigs a category contains. I will tell you which category exactly each kind of gig I suggest should be in, in the next chapter.

The most in-demand categories on Fiverr, in the order of most searched to least, at the time of writing this ebook are: Online Marketing, Graphics & Design, Advertising, Video & Animation and Writing & Translation.

## COVER PHOTO

This is a special section when creating a gig that is not available for most categories. You are able to upload a "Facebook timeline-like" cover photo that becomes a full-page banner across the top of your gig. What you upload depends on what you're selling. If you're selling yourself, say holding a sign or making a video testimonial, you should upload a photo of yourself showing off your personality. A large photo of you standing in front of the Eiffel Tower or photo of you in the middle of a food fight. Something like this makes your gigs more personable and fun. It gives your customers comfort and a feeling like they know you.

If you're selling a thing, like graphics or jewelry, then the cover photo should obviously be of your product. High quality photos are highly recommended.

Put effort into it, don't be lazy and do a Google Images search. Either buy a gig from someone on Fiverr to make you a great looking cover photo or make one yourself if you have the ability. **Always upload a cover photo** if you are using a category that allows cover photo uploads.

Take a look at the top sellers on the front page to see what their cover photos look like. (A lot of Top Rated Sellers are still not taking advantage of this new feature, you should!) Here are a few examples of ones I like and you should try to emulate:

You are able to upload a cover photo for the following gig categories: Fun & Bizarre, Graphics & Design, Advertising, Lifestyle, Gifts, and Video & Animation.

## GIG GALLERY

Here you upload photos relevant to your gig. This is not as important as you might think. In the "Secret Sauce" section of this chapter, I will tell you why the Gig Gallery is not going to make or break your earnings. The most important part of creating your gig is the secret sauce. But for now, let me break down how to properly use the gig gallery.

The gig gallery allows you to upload JPEGs no bigger than 5 MB. The recommended dimensions for these photos are 682x459, I know those are weird dimensions but that's what Fiverr recommends and scales your images to.

Here you should only use high quality photos. Either samples of your work, like if you're selling logo designs for example, pictures of yourself if you're going to be modeling a sign or doing video testimonials, or an image created by you or someone else which attractively displays the service you offer, like a splash image advertising your backlinks service. You can either make that kind of image yourself or again, find someone on Fiverr to do it.

You don't want it to be something made in paint or cheap looking. Your image has to look fantastic and dimensioned properly. This helps with conversions. Here's an image for SEO services that I think is a good example:

## GIG META DETA

The new Gig Meta Data allows buyers to define their gigs much more specifically than before.

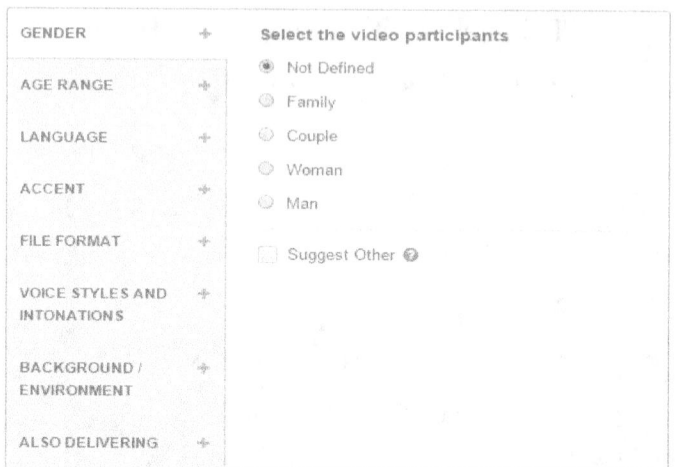

Above is an example of Gig Meta Data for a gig created under VIDEO & ANIMATION > TESTIMONIALS & REVIEWS BY ACTORS.

There are a lot of options to choose from. Most metadata sections only allow for you to choose one option. If you want to choose more than one option, I would suggest creating separate gigs for each option. If you feel the need to select several options, that might tell you that you're better off creating different gigs for each option. Not only will that allow you to rank better for searchs, but it will also give you more opportunity to be found by buyers. More gigs, more opportunities to be found.

## GIG VIDEO - THE SECRET SAUCE (PART 1)

Okay, so here's the big secret sauce and the main thing that will help get you more sales than you currently are. **You must upload a video for all your gigs**. Period. Fiverr is not lying when they say gigs sell better when they have a video. Your gig will appear higher in searches.

I know, what you're thinking... *"That's* the secret sauce? That's it?" Well, there's actually a little more to it. There's also a secret ingredient to it. Keep reading!

You would be shocked as to how many sellers do not upload a video for their gigs. Even the successfully selling gigs would do twice as much in sales if they just had a video.

The biggest thing I found experimenting with Fiverr, and that I never see anyone ever suggest, is something so simple. You need a video for all your gigs. And yes, it doesn't even matter what you're selling, you should create and upload a video for your gigs.

If you're not camera shy, I recommend you record yourself. You can use a digital camera or even a webcam/camera phone if the quality is decent enough. You can use a free video editing software like Windows Movie Maker or something like Camtasia to edit the video if needed to add some background music or graphics. Again, you can pay someone on Fiverr to edit your video if you have no experience with this.

Sit in front of the camera, under some good lighting, and read off of a script. Keep it short and simple. Say it like you're talking to a friend. Don't be shy and give it a few takes. Here's a sample script if you were to sell Twitter followers:

*"Hey, I'm Gianluca! Do you like Twitter followers?*

*I can get you over 1000 high quality Twitter followers for only five bucks, exclusively here on Fiverr! My services are fast and safe! Try me out! You guys won't be disappointed! Thanks!"*

On the video itself, I'd place a little Twitter graphic so people can see the Twitter logo in the video thumbnail. In the video itself, I'd put some cool, royalty free music (search YouTube for "royalty free music" and download it).

You need to be careful though. Lately, Fiverr have been **very strict**

when it comes to moderating and deciding what videos are allowed on gigs.

The two biggest things, it seems, is you must state your gig is "exclusively on Fiverr" and you must have good audio and video quality. Any videos which are out of sync or have poor lighting will be rejected. It's also good practice to introduce yourself, something like "Hi, my name is     "

For some reason though, these rules are not shown on their website and you will go through a lot of rejections without reason unless you know what they are. Here are their rules:

- Video duration must be over 10 seconds and up to 30 seconds.
- Use only original videos made by you.

- Upload a video of yourself presenting your own gig. You may include samples of your work, editing effects etc. as long as the presentation remains personal and made by you
- Mention that your gig is offered exclusively on fiverr.com
- Do not use the same video for more than one gig
- Your video must be in reasonable quality, your voice has to be clear and easy to understand
- Promotion of third party services, websites or brands (in writing or narration) or providing a direct means of communication will not be allowed
- Offering a service for any price other than $5 is not allowed
- Make sure your video and gig adheres with our Terms of Service.
- Videos related to self improvement, getting rich methods, black hat marketing and similar are not permitted at this time.

We will be breaking the "Use only original videos made by you rule" later. Don't worry, do it right and Fiverr will not be able to tell.


Check out some of the videos of gigs on the first page for more ideas. You don't have to look like a model for this to help you get more sales. (Well, a little bit more on that later) This helps as it ranks you better in searches (a lot better), places you higher in category pages, it makes your gigs appear more trustworthy (you are putting yourself in front of a camera after all) and it gives your gigs personality (I'm going to buy Twitter followers from the guy with the cool voice and moustache!)

Another thing to consider is that Fiverr **loves** gigs with videos like this.

They eat it up. Why should you care? If your gigs have personality and videos like this, they have a much better chance of showing up on the front page and featured or, better yet, make you a Top Rated Seller.

If this doesn't click with you, you'll just have to trust me on this. The culture and environment on Fiverr is not just some faceless marketplace. The whole idea is you're paying a real person for a small service or product. Someone with a picture, biography, personality and video of themselves. If you keep your profile and gigs faceless, you will be buried under thousands of other faceless gigs. If you haven't tried this yet, do it and I guarantee you will see a huge difference in your sales.

Which gig are you more likely to click on for the exact same service?

I will drive UNLIMITED genuine real traffic to your website for one m...

I will drive UNLIMITED genuine real traffic to your website for one m...

If you're too camera shy, there is a second option. It's not as good, but it will help since you will have at least a video on all your gigs. You can upload an animated video that describes your gig. You can either hire someone on Fiverr or use a site like Wideo.co or VideoScribe which lets you make animated videos with zero animating skills or knowledge.

**There's another element to this though. <u>A secret ingredient</u> to this secret sauce to help your gigs sell even more.** It's a little shallow, and it pretty much relies on the old adage "sex sells". Instead of using yourself in your video or creating an animated video, **you're going to hire a beautiful young woman (or young man) to be a spokesperson for your gigs**.

If you are an attractive and charismatic person, you will save yourself time and money by just using yourself in your videos. If you don't think you are, hire someone (although, you don't need to be a model or superstar to simply make a video of yourself talking about your gig!). There are different places you can go to hire an actress or actor (I prefer an actress) to be a spokesperson for your gig. The first way, is the obvious one: hire a person on Fiverr. This is risky though, Fiverr will eventually see that the video is not of you and take the video down. So the best way is to hire someone outside of Fiverr, where they won't be able to link it or figure it out, this is what I did. You can post a classified on Craigslist or Kijiji, or post an ad in a Facebook group that is for models looking for work.

The title of your ad should be something like "Looking for actress to be spokesperson for my service, make me 30 second video from home". You'll usually have to pay around $20 for each video, it's not as cheap as Fiverr but you will make that money back. In the body of the ad, be sure to state "no previous acting experience required, sample video preferred, must at least provide a photo." When you hire someone, give them a script in the first-person. Something like:

"Hi, I'm Shelly, [give them the option to use their own name or a fake name] I'm here to design you a logo for your small business or website for only five bucks exclusively here on Fiverr! Take a look at my portfolio for some samples of my work on my gig page below.

I'm fast and guarantee a high quality logo!"

This way, it will appear as though you are that girl selling your gigs on Fiverr. The more attractive and charming the actor/actress is, the better the result. From my experience, I've found the gigs I've had with an attractive actress have always brought me the most gig orders.

On my very first Fiverr account, I had about 1-3 orders a day, if that, for my first few months. I decided to change things up and I found an attractive actress to do 6 videos for 6 of my gigs. After uploading these videos to my gigs, not only did I find I was getting more orders but I was also getting more page views. It seemed like Fiverr was placing my gigs higher on category pages.

## DESCRIPTION

Obviously, this is dependent on what you're selling. So, in the next chapter, I will tell you what description to put for each gig I suggest. However, in general, you want to stuff as many keywords as possible in your descriptions. Fiverr will not allow you to publish your gig if it contains too many instances of a keyword, so just put as many as Fiverr will allow.

Usually it's 3 instances.

You also only have 1200 characters to work with. While that may seem like a lot, I generally like to have a FAQ in my descriptions after I describe the gig. Trust me, when you get 30-40 orders a day, you won't want to deal with the same questions over and over as well as the same mistakes people make when ordering your gig, such as assuming you do something you don't.

The first part of your description should be straight to the point. It's basically you taking your title of your gig, but putting the full length version of your title you couldn't fit in the title because of the character limit. A good place to start if you sell Twitter followers would be something like: "1000 high quality Twitter followers fast to any profile. No account access required, all real-looking and 100% safe".

I recommend bolding this and even highlighting it. The next section could be bullet points, breaking down all the features of your gig, or exactly everything they get for $5.

Lastly, try to fit in a FAQ if you can. I like to put disclaimers here and answer common questions I get.

## TAGS

These are very important if you want your gig to be picked up in searches. You're only allowed a maximum of 5 keywords here so make them good. You're also only allowed to use a keyword once. So if I use "Twitter" I can't also put "Twitter followers". So which do you use? Put the keywords people are searching. Fiverr users are not really searching "Twitter", they're using "Twitter followers" so use that as a keyword instead of just "Twitter".

What I like to do, is put relevant keywords here so I'm picked up in searches where users may not be exactly looking for my service, but when they see it, they think "Oh, I could use that too" or "Let me check this out".

Using the Twitter followers example again, I will obviously

use the keywords "Twitter followers, real, fast" but I'll also throw in "retweets" and "favorites" even though my gig is only selling followers. This way, I'll be picked up in searches where users are seeking retweets and favorites.

They're still likely to view my gig since they would likely want followers too. I will help you further with this concept in the next chapter but you will need to think outside the box.

## PRICE

Some gigs categories allow for Gig Packages. This allows you to charge more than $5 for your gigs. This was introduced as a new selling feature in late 2015. Fiverr plans to roll out Gig Packages to all categories. To learn more about it, visit their blog.

## DELIVERY TIME

The delivery time of your gig is purely dependent on a few things. If you have a supplier or are outsourcing something, test your supplier first before making a gig. See how long it takes them to deliver on average. I go into this a bit in my next chapter but that is one way to determine duration so your orders don't end up being late.

If you're selling video testimonials or photos of yourself holding a sign, put 1 day in the very beginning, especially if you're not even a level 1 seller. This will require work in the beginning, but once you get at least 10 orders and positive reviews, you can always change this to 2 or 3 days and have an Express gig extra where you will deliver this in 1 day. I go into having a 1 day gig duration in a future chapter and how this can help sky rocket your sales when you have a new gig or account.

Even if your gig is running late, Fiverr allows you an additional 24 hours to deliver the gig before the seller is able to cancel. So, you technically have 2 days to deliver a gig even when you set it to 1 day. If you're running really late, <u>always</u> notify your buyer or ask your buyer to "please not cancel the order". **This is key**. If you've already outsourced the gig and paid someone else and your buyer cancels, you will lose that money. On top of that, **negative feedback is left whenever a buyer cancels a late order!**

So be careful.

## REQUIREMENTS

If you don't have this part set-up right, expect to get a lot of orders that will end up being a headache. The key here is to ask for every single thing you need, no matter how obvious you think it is. You'd be surprised, people will order a gig like Twitter followers and then assume you're a psychic and just *know* what their Twitter account is. So, don't leave anything out. Here's a good template to start from:

"HEY! Thanks for your business :) Please provide me with _____ Also include

-_

Please no requests after ordering. Everything I provide is as per my gig description!

If you like____you should check out my other gig linktogigorwebsite.com"

Your "Instructions to buyers" also allow you to **cross-promote other gigs** of yours. I go into this in detail in chapter 5. Because of the character limits, don't be afraid to click "Add another requirement" for each Gig extra you offer if necessary. Fiverr allows for you to have multiple different instructions for buyers. This allows you to have optional instructions for buyers if they order any of your Gig extras.

# CHAPTER 4:

## WHAT TO SELL ON FIVERR; MINIMUM WORK FOR MAXIMUM EARNINGS

I will now go over, in detail, which kinds of gigs to sell on Fiverr, how to sell them, and where to outsource if required. When outsourcing, maximum you should spend per order is $1. That will leave you with $3 profit since Fiverr also takes $1. This may not seem like a lot at first, but with enough volume (20+ orders a day) and enough gig multiples and gig extras ordered, you can be making at least $2000 a month initially.

Before getting excited and using one of these gig suggestions immediately, be sure to read the previous chapter in which I described in detail exactly how to create a gig that will get the most traffic possible as well as the most sales. It isn't only about what you sell but also how you describe it, title it, what keywords you use, what pictures/videos to use and more.

### SEO SERVICES

Search Engine Optimization services are in high demand on Fiverr.

Many users come to Fiverr looking for cheap backlinks or an affordable way to help rank their websites or their client's websites. This is an excellent gig to provide even if you have little to no experience when it comes to SEO.

Backlinks, directory submissions, backlink indexing, blog comments, article submissions and search engine submission are all things that are highly searched and purchased on Fiverr. Don't be overwhelmed by the amount of competition in this category on Fiverr. You can still make decent coin reselling these services. Remember, the reason there's competition in anything is because there is a demand and it sells. Competition is good. It means it will work.

To do this, you will need a supplier. To find a supplier, I recommend SEO Clerks. There are many other ways to find a supplier or a service to resell, but I find SEO Clerks to be the simplest and easiest. I personally don't care nor think it matters where you find a supplier. I only care that it is quality, reliable, and cheap.

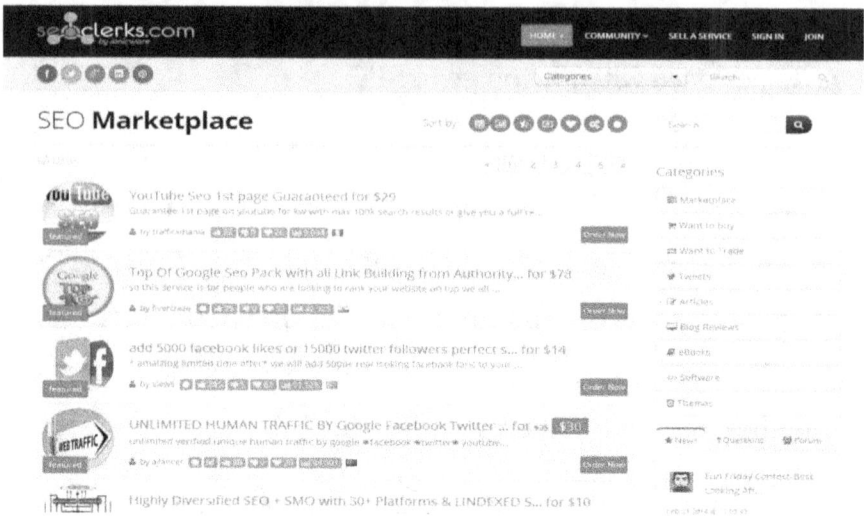

SEO Clerks is a site much like Fiverr. You can find all kinds of services for as little as $1. The plan is to look for great $1 SEO services and resell them on Fiverr for $5. So, go ahead and create an account on SEO Clerks by clicking "Join" on the upper-right hand corner of the page. I would not recommend registering the same username as your Fiverr username in case a savvy Fiverr user Googles your Fiverr username since your SEO Clerks account may appear in the searches.

Now, on the main page, on the right sidebar you will see Marketplace.

Click that and the sidebar will expand to show all the categories. The categories we want, as SEO resellers, are: Blackhat/Bulk Links, Directory Submission, Link Building, and Traffic.

To figure out which services on SEO Clerks to resell, we need to first pick a category. Let's click on Blackhat/Bulk Links. After clicking the link, at the top of the page you will see "Sort by:" We want to sort all these services by Price.

Now, you will see all the services that are listed for $1. How do we choose from this massive list of services? Choose one that has a lot of thumbs up, and a lot of views. This one looks good:

do drip feed and keyword diversity 5 PR2 - PR5 blog comments... for $1
We are feeling proud to announce new version for this service, version [v 2.0] is avail...

by ITKING  815  0  106  41,282          Order Now

Take a look at the reviews and comments, the expected delivery time and the average delivery time. If these things all look good and the seller is active (he or she has a review within the last few days) go ahead and test the supplier. You should always test the supplier before using them to resell a gig on Fiverr. This will give you an idea of the quality of their service, the speed, and the quality of their communication.

Once you select a supplier or a few services to resell, it's important to not be tempted to use the exact gig titles, descriptions and images that they use for their gigs. Fiverr's character and keyword limits are different and you also are going to want to describe the gig in the best way so that it will get the most conversions.

Be sure to bookmark this seller's gig page as you will come back to it often to buy gigs to resell. You want to save as much time as possible.

**Gig Title:** Do not copy your supplier's title word for word. Remember to follow the guidelines from the previous chapter. Use the most important keywords in your title that users seek such as "Penguin friendly" when you can fit it.

**Category:** "Online Marketing > SEO" "Online Marketing > Bookmarking & Links" "Online Marketing > Other"

**Gig Description:** Again, very important, do not copy your supplier's description word for word. Include the features of your gig that your supplier offers and any important disclaimers to protect yourself and your gig.

**Gig Gallery:** Do not take or use the image your supplier uses. Either pay someone on Fiverr to make you a simple image or make one yourself. Have fun with it. You can also be cliché too since that will catch people's eyes. If you're providing a service that will increase someone's Google ranking, you can include a rocket next to Google's logo. You can also include screenshots here showing rank changes.

You can use Google images to search for "serp ranking result" to find a few graphs showing increases in ranking of specific keywords after a few weeks.

**Gig Video:** So, firstly, follow my instructions from the previous chapter on this topic. Remember, your video is VERY important and it's critical you have one. Be authoritative in your videos, or make sure your spokesperson is. Act like you know what you're talking about. You can talk in front of a whiteboard or have graphs floating around in your video. You can also keep it simple and talk to the camera in your computer chair with a laptop in the background showing Google or some Google Analytics.

**Duration:** If your supplier has an average delivery date of 3 days, you should use 4. This provides a nice buffer. This will give you 5 days to complete the order since Fiverr gives you an additional 24 hours when your gig is late.

Tags: SEO, SERPS increase, Google ranking, panda safe, penguin safe, backlinks, quality backlinks, safe backlinks, Google first page, SEO articles, keywords.

**Instructions to buyers:** Whatever your supplier asks from you, you should ask the same thing from Fiverr users. Use the template from the last chapter. This is also a great opportunity to cross-promote a keyword research gig (gig described later in this chapter).

## IDEAS FOR GIG EXTRAS:

**Express gig extra:** Depending on the duration of your supplier, you can offer an express gig extra which changes the duration time of your gig to a shorter duration time that you choose. I recommend charging

$5 for this. It's a very tempting gig extra for many users and keeping the price low will give you a much higher conversion. I find about 1 out of 6 of my sales will order the Express gig extra. Some suppliers and sellers on SEO Clerks offer an option for a faster delivery, so this can help you as well decide the duration for the Express gig extra.

**Offer whatever else that same supplier offers for $1:** Check that seller's profile, see if they offer any other services for a $1 that are relevant and include that as a gig extra.

**EDU domain backlinks:** You can sell these as a gig extra to add-on to your backlinks gig. Lots of users seek .EDU backlinks since they are much harder to acquire and help a lot with SEO.

**Offer a package:** If your standard gig sells 1000 backlinks for $5, offer a gig extra that sells 2500 for $5. Offer your customers some savings in the gig extras to encourage more users to spend more than just $5. If you offer value in your gig extras, you will see your average selling price on Fiverr go up. You could also resell a more expensive SEO Clerks gig here. If there's a backlink package on SEO Clerks for $20, sell it here for $40 or however much you think it would sell for. Make sure the margin of profit is worth selling.

## Social Media Traffic / Social Signals

A lot of people come to Fiverr looking to boost their Twitter followers or get more Facebook likes and shares on their website. You could easily take advantage of this demand by finding a supplier and outsource these jobs.

Using SEO Clerks again from the "SEO SERVICES" section of this e- book, you can find many people offering Twitter, Instagram, Facebook, Vine, YouTube, and Pinterest services for as low as $1.

On the right sidebar of SEO Clerks, click Marketplace and select the category "Social Networks". Like in the previous section, we want to sort by price and find a member who offers a service with a lot of thumbs up ratings and views. This one is a good example:

Add Over 1,300 High quality Twitter Followers Without Admin ... for $1
1,000 facebook fanpage like $1 add over 1,300 high quality staying twitter followers...

by sarower 269 3 22 720,644

Order Now

As before, you will want to test out the supplier, but with your own social media accounts or with social media accounts you control. This way you can see the quality of the followers or likes, or check the analytics of your video if it's a YouTube service.

When I first wrote this book back in late-2017, these gigs sold like hot cakes. Now, Fiverr has begun cracking down on them so unfortunately, while these gigs will likely do very well for you, eventually, Fiverr will suspend these gigs it seems. I left this in the book when I updated it just because I still think it's a very useful section and could still be sold on Fiverr if you title your gigs clever enough that it isn't completely obvious what you're selling.

**Gig Title:** I go over this in my last chapter regarding this gig type, but just to go over it briefly, don't copy your supplier's title word for word and be sure to include as many frequently searched words as possible while keeping the title short and sweet to make it rank better on Fiverr. Again, to keep your gig out of Fiverr's crosshairs, come up with a clever title. "I will get you Twitter fans" "I will make you popular on Twitter".

**Category:** "Online Marketing > Social Marketing" "Online Marketing

> Get Traffic" "Online Marketing > Video Marketing" for YouTube services

**Gig Description:** Highlight the major features of your service. Be sure to include keywords like "real, quality, safe" if you can. I wouldn't suggest advertising your followers or subscribers as real when they're not. It's okay though to put "real looking" or "real quality". I will admit advertising as real in the title and description WILL get you more sales. In the long run though, people will bust you if they're clever enough. It's better to just be honest off the bat. People can't buy real Twitter followers but they can get really good looking fakes. Another smart thing to include is an FAQ. Address the common questions like "Are they real?" "Can you provide X from only Y country?"

"How fast do the followers/subscribers/likes/whatever come?" You will save yourself many unneeded messages in your inbox and many hours of answering questions to people who will likely not buy anyway.

**Gig Gallery:** Don't steal an image that your supplier uses. Create your own, something simple, in Photoshop if you're competent, if not pay someone on Fiverr to make you one. This is not that important though. The video is much more important. You could also put screenshots showing samples of your work. So, if you're selling Twitter followers, take screenshots of sample accounts that you sent followers to showing Fiverr buyers what the followers look like.

**Gig Video:** Your video should contain a logo in the corner of the screen of the logo of the social media site you're providing a service for. So whether it's a video of yourself or a video of a female spokesperson you paid, it's important to have so that when Fiverr users see the thumbnail of your gig, they will see either a Twitter logo or YouTube logo next to you in your thumbnail, catching their eye.

Other than this, follow instructions and tips in the previous chapter to ensure your video is optimized for conversions.

**Duration:** If your supplier has an average delivery date of 3 days, you should use 4. This provides a nice buffer. This will give you 5 days to complete the order since Fiverr gives you an additional 24 hours when your gig is late.

**Tags:** Remember to include the complete tag. So, if your gig is YouTube views, the keyword should be "YouTube views" not "YouTube", "Views". Also include other keywords many users search for when looking for social media services and social signals: real, quality, fast, followers, safe, SEO, etc. Remember to include relevant keywords to catch people who are making relevant searches. So, if you're selling YouTube views, also include the keywords "Likes" "Subscribers" even if you're not providing those as gig extras.

**Instructions to buyers:** Whatever your supplier asks from you, you should ask the same thing from Fiverr users. Use the template from the last chapter. Include multiple instructions if your gig extras require different information.

## IDEAS FOR GIG EXTRAS:

**Express gig extra:** It depends how fast your supplier can deliver the gig or if your supplier offers an extra to have the order processed faster.

**Followers/Likes:** If you sell Twitter followers, use

Retweets or Favorites as a gig extra. If you sell Instagram Likes, use Instagram followers. If you sell YouTube views, sell subscribers as a gig extra.

## VIDEOSCRIBE/WHITEBOARD ANIMATIONS

Videoscribe animations and whiteboard animations have become a very popular trend over the past year and it seems more and more small businesses are using these on their websites. If you haven't seen them before, they are videos where an animated hand will rapidly write and draw along with a narration usually to describe a service or product in an entertaining manner. If you'd like to see a sample of this on YouTube, here's one I found.

Now, you might look at this and think "wow that looks really complicated" but it's really not. There's software that allows you to make whiteboard animations in a short amount of time. The most popular software available for this is VideoScribe. They have an online utility that allows you to make whiteboard animations as well as save them on their site. Even if you have no experience using graphic design software or video animating software, VideoScribe is very user friendly and easy to use. Plus, it's risk free as they give you a trial to try out their software on their site which is what I did to see if it'd be something I could quickly learn. This is something you could learn to do in a weekend and make a lot of money since it is something extremely desirable right now, especially on Fiverr.

They provide a large library of music, graphics and fonts to make your job even easier. VideoScribe is $17 USD a month but it quickly pays itself off after you see how in demand this gig is. One of the most successful Top Rated Sellers on Fiverr only sells video scribe animations to give you an idea of how well these gigs sell.

VideoScribe      Scribe wall    Help    Free trial    Pricing    SPARKOL    Account

Whiteboard video inspiration from around the world. Some full of fancy, some technically cunning, some the essence of fun. All made with VideoScribe.

If you're afraid that this software is too much work or too difficult to use, watch this 13 minute tutorial on making your first whiteboard animation.

**Gig Title:** Remember to keep it brief to rank better in searches. A good title would be something like "create a whiteboard animation digital hand drawn video scribe". This catches all the keywords as usually people who search for this gig will either search for it as a whiteboard animation, hand drawn animation or video scribe. You cover all your bases here.

**Category:** "Video & Animation > Animation & 3D"

**Cover photo:** Either create a 1100x260 banner or hire someone on Fiverr to make one for you cheap. I recommend something clever like a large whiteboard with doodles and logos on it.

**Gig Description:** This depends purely on the amount of

work you're willing to do for $5. I recommend offering a 60 second animation, up to 90 words, and with 4 total images including their logo. It's also very important to highlight and bold that people must contact you first for a quote if their animation will be longer or requires more images. This way, you won't get orders from people who just want to know how much their project costs. Lastly, be sure to state you only provide one revision if required and the revisions must be within reason. Make it clear they're already getting a high quality animation for only $5.

**Gig Gallery:** I'd recommend taking a screenshot of one of your video scribe animations and using that with a caption like "Exclusively on Fiverr for only $5". This isn't as important

**Gig Video:** Remember when you deliver orders to use the videos in your showcase to show your work. The main gig video itself should be a video animation you make yourself. What I like to do is make a video scribe describing your gig as well as using the Fiverr logo.

**Duration:** A good duration is about 5 days to give yourself a buffer in case you receive many orders or if you cannot begin the animation right away. This allows you to have an Express gig extra too for the impatient buyers who can't wait 5 days.

**Tags:** "whiteboard" "videoscribe" "animation" "hand drawn" "logo" are the good ones. You could also add "white board" "video scribe" too.

**Instructions to buyers:** "Thank you for your order. Please provide me with the text (up to 90 words) for your 60 second animation. Please attach any graphics and logos you wish to have as well" "Please no requests outside of what I offer! You must ask for a quote before ordering if this is the case."

## IDEAS FOR GIG EXTRAS:

**Express gig extra:** If you are able to complete a video in 24 hours, charge $20. Otherwise, I'd recommend a $5-$10 extra to have the video completed in 2 days.

**Sync your 60 second voice over with animation:** You could also make this gig extra "Provide you with a voice over" if you are confident/skilled enough and have a good microphone. Otherwise, charge $10 to allow your buyer to attach an .mp3 voice over which you will animate to in VideoScribe.

**Deliver your animation in HD:** This is no additional work for you or any special process on VideoScribe, but why not charge more for it? It can bring up the average gig selling price for you. Charge $5.

## ARTICLE WRITING/SPINNING

A lot of website owners come to Fiverr looking for cheap content for their websites or blogs. This helps with SEO on their websites or simply filling up new websites with content. It's one of the more in-demand gigs on Fiverr and a lot of Top Rated

Sellers sell written content. One Top Rated Seller's article writing gig has received **over 22,000 orders**!

You can go different ways with this. You can actually write up articles of any topic for your buyers (this is a lot of work) or use a program which will "spin" or rewrite articles for you that is readable and passes any plagiarism checker. I prefer the latter. It's a lot easier and you can provide more content for $5 faster. If you wish to actually write the content yourself from scratch, I suggest offering a lower word count than what is suggested in this book. I would suggest a 300 word count gig for an article written by you.

Again, I don't suggest this as this is a lot of work especially if you are asked to write about a topic you are not familiar with at all or requires time- intensive research. The best way to do this gig is to spin articles from the internet.

The best article spinner or rewriter on the market is WordAI. Nothing compares. A lot of other software that spins articles simply use a basic thesaurus to find synonyms to many of the words but these articles will wind up being barely readable and require a lot of work on your part to correct them. WordAI spins the articles you provide it in a way that it is still readable and looks like it was written by human. The most important part is that these articles pass CopyScape or other plagiarism checkers to ensure Google won't detect your articles as duplicate content.

Many Top Rated Sellers, including myself, have seen a lot of success doing this. I've personally used WordAI to rewrite articles and I would suggest it as everything else I've used was not producing the quality I liked. WordAI is 50 USD a month and very much worth it considering it is the hands-down best and most human-like spinner on the market. WordAI also allows a 3 days trial, so you can try it out for yourself to see how easy it is.

It's very easy to do and it will only take you 5-10 minutes (at the very most) per article if you use WordAI. The first thing is you need an article to spin. Use an article directory such as ezinearticles to find an article on the topic your buyer requests. For example, if your buyer is looking for an article on "dog grooming" simply search for that topic to find many articles covering that topic. Choose from any of them (preferably ones with around 500 word count) and copy the content.

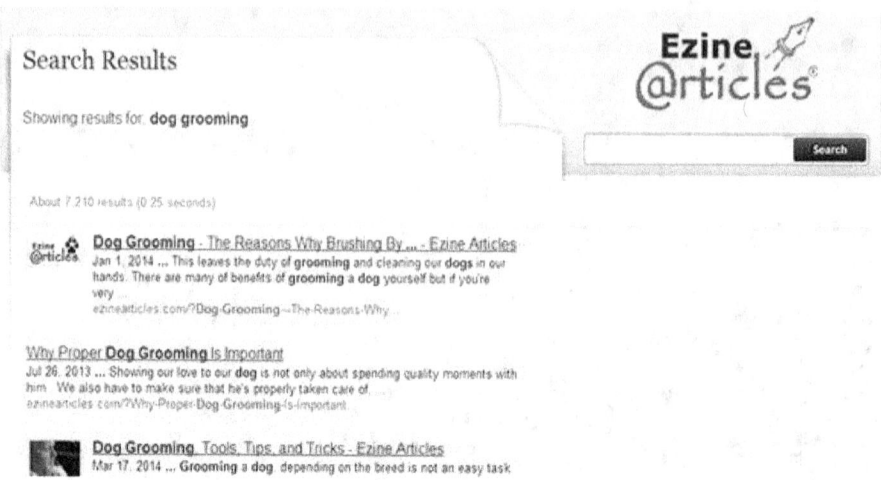

Go to WordAI or the spinner of your choice and paste the content. With WordAI you simply copy and paste the content into the spinner. Before spinning, it will ask you for the "spinning quality", you want it to be readable. The more readable it is, the less spinning WordAI will do and the more likely it will be perceived as duplicate content by Google.

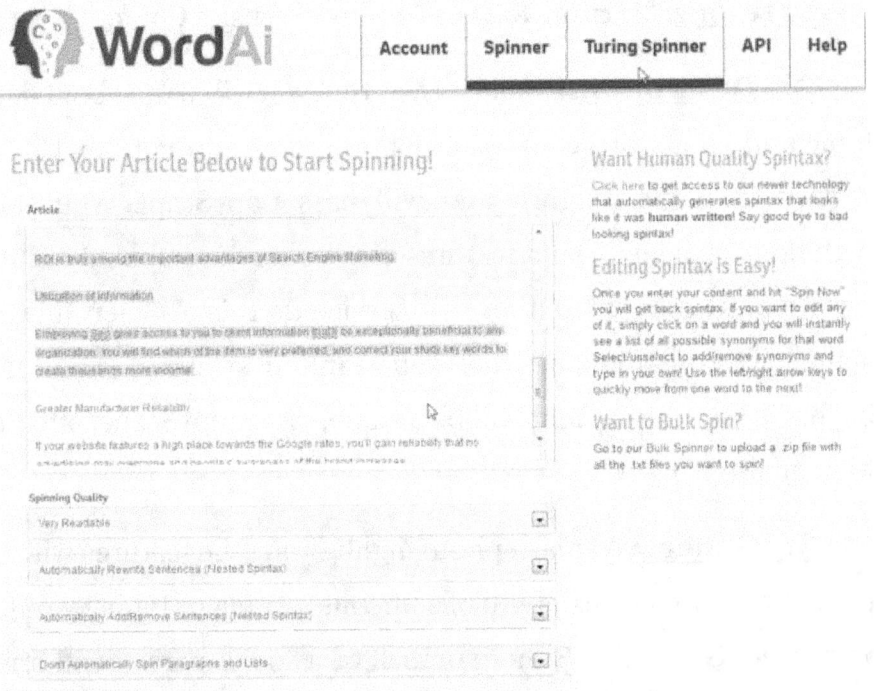

After you spin the article, read it over to make sure it makes sense. It may require some fine tuning. The technology is not perfect but it's pretty good and a lot faster and easier than writing an article from scratch.

After editing, I highly recommend using a plagiarism checker, either a free one or a paid one like CopyScape.

**Gig Title:** Again, remember to keep it brief to rank better in searches. Here are some sample titles: "write a 400 word article" "write original content up to 500 words for your website" "write SEO optimized content up to 500 words" "write a quality article that passes CopyScape 500 words"

**Category:** "Writing & Translation > Website Content"

**Gig Description:** Make it clear that you will write about any topic and your word count is strict. Make sure to note that it is written in native English and will pass CopyScape. You can highlight the benefits and features of your service in bullet point. I see many sellers who offer this service do this, to keep things simple. Overall though, what you want to stress to potential buyers is that the content will be unique, pass CopyScape, and be high quality.

**Gig Gallery:** A splash photo highlighting the features with a photo of you or a stock photo of someone writing or typing would work well. Gig Video: Either yourself or a spokesperson you hire talking about the features of your gig. Make sure to include "Exclusively here on Fiverr" somewhere in your gig. A video for this gig is very important as most sellers do not bother with a video for their article writing gigs. This will help you significantly when it comes to appearing in searches or under the Writing category on Fiverr.

**Duration:** Most sellers offer a 3 day duration. I would recommend 3 to 5 days.

**Tags:** "writer" "website" "content" "article" "post" are the best keywords for this gig.

**Instructions to buyers:** Ask for the topic of the article, let your buyers know the more general the topic is the better, and to include any keywords if you are offering SEO optimized articles.

## IDEAS FOR GIG EXTRAS:

**Express gig extra:** Offer to write the article in 24 hours for $10.

**Package it, 5 articles for the price of 4:** Charge $15 for this gig extra (it will be $20 total) and offer your buyers 5 total articles.

**SEO Optimized:** You can include this as a gig extra and promise to include keywords they desire into the article. If you are familiar with long tail keywords, you can offer this gig extra. I would charge $5 for this.

### KEYWORD/NICHE RESEARCH

Keyword research entails looking at a long tail keyword or a group of keywords such as "horse back riding in Canada" and getting a list of relevant keywords as well as how competitive they are, how many searches they receive a month, how easy they are to rank for and more. A lot of sellers provide this service and almost all of them use the same software to easily research any keyword and export the results to a nice Excel file.

You don't even need to be an SEO expert or really even know what you're doing. All you need is the keyword or niche your buyer wants you to research, enter it into the software, and it will give you all the data you need to send to your buyer. If you haven't noticed by now, you will see a lot of the methods I offer in this e-book cater to small businesses. This isn't a coincidence; this is where the demand comes from: small business and website owners looking to outsource work for cheap.

I and many sellers use Long Tail Pro. It's very easy to use and not only is it powerful and great for personal use, it's a great way to make some money on Fiverr.

All you need to do is log into your Google account, that has AdSense setup, into the program's settings. Once this is done, you're pretty much set. Type in a keyword (preferably a long tail keyword) and click "Add".

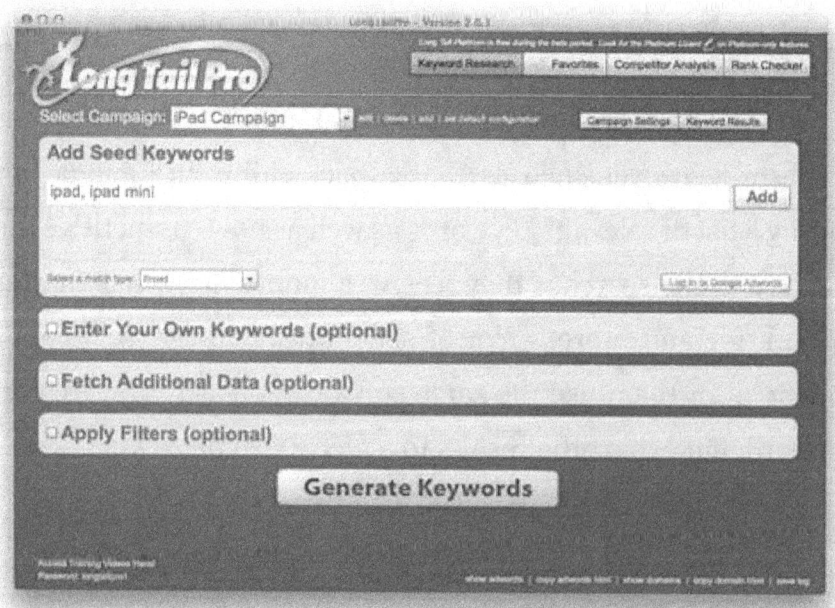

The software will do its thing and output a list of similar keywords that get searches as well as show the number of searches per month, the "Cost per Click" for websites that use this keyword will earn from AdSense, the number of results, the difficulty to rank for this keyword and the availability of the domains for this keyword.

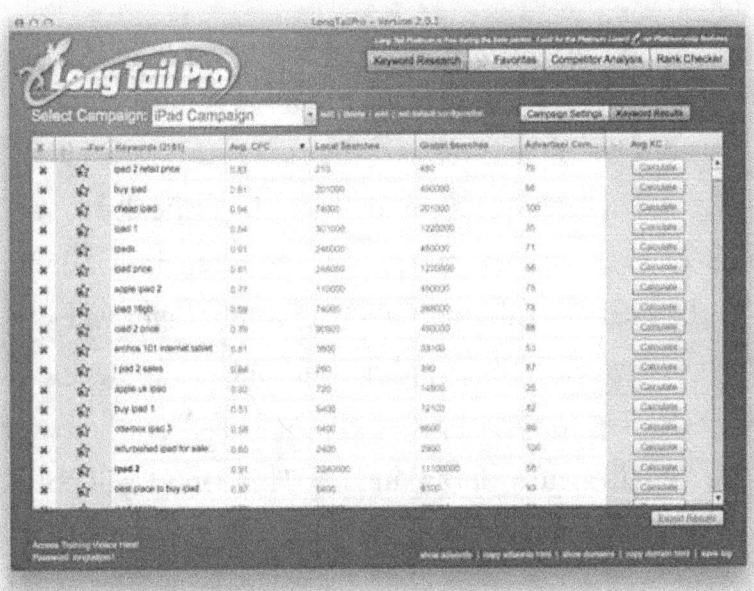

Check the domains and competition for the keywords that get the most searches and simply export the results to an Excel file and deliver to your buyer. It's really that easy. If you want you can edit the Excel file and personalize it a little, include your buyer's information, username and even your own logo. There are tons of software that can do this but I find Long Tail Pro to be the best and easiest to use. It's $97 USD but it's only a one- time cost and includes a 60 day guarantee so if you don't make your money back or don't like the software, you could simply get a refund. Plus, there's a 10 day trial available so you can try out and learn the software, just to see how powerful it actually is.

**Gig Title:** "do keyword research for your niche or business" "do in- depth SEO keyword research for your niche"

**Category:** "Online Marketing > Keywords Research"

**Gig Description:** "I will find the best keywords for your niche or business. I will provide a detailed report with a list of relevant keywords as well as their monthly searches. Each keyword will also show its competition, its difficulty to rank for, number of backlinks of the top website, domain availability as well as the Cost Per Click earned from AdSense for websites that use this keyword. This report will help you decide which keywords to try to rank on Google for based on their monthly searches and difficulty of ranking for. This report will potentially help you find untapped keywords that are easy to rank for but receive a lot of searches and are relevant to your niche or business."

**Gig Gallery:** A photo sample of an Excel file with data or even just a picture of yourself with a Google logo or a bunch of keywords splashed behind you. Your gig gallery can also include screenshots of Excel files but I wouldn't recommend taking a screenshot of the software itself.

**Gig Video:** You should either have yourself or someone you hire in front of the camera describing your gig. As always, include that this gig is exclusively on Fiverr. You can highlight all of the features of this gig from the description above as well as include some graphics like a collage of keywords or Google's logo.

**Duration:** Most sellers offer a 3 day duration. I would recommend 3 to 5 days, but you could start at 24 hours to kick start some sales in the beginning as this is very easy and quick to deliver.

**Tags:** "keyword research" "niche" "SEO optimization" "rank website" "Google"

**Instructions to buyers:** Ask for the specific niche or even a link to their website. Also ask for a specific keyword they're trying to rank for. This is also a great opportunity to cross-promote your SEO gigs if you have any.

## IDEAS FOR GIG EXTRAS:

**Express gig extra:** Offer to do the research in 1 day for $5-$10. Experiment with the price, I personally think $5 works best, as you'll see more people purchase it.

**Package a SEO service:** You can include backlinks or whatever other SEO gig you sell for $5. You could even resell a more expensive SEO gig from SEO Clerks here.

**VIDEO TESTIMONIALS AND SPOKESPERSON / HOLD YOUR SIGN**

This is a very popular gig to start your Fiverr career off with that is very easy to do if you have the confidence to sit in front of a camera. Many of the more popular or famous Top Rated Sellers on Fiverr do this.

It's very simple: offer the buyer a video where you will look into the camera and either provide a testimonial for their product/service or be the spokesperson for their business or website. All you need is a decent camera that records in HD. It doesn't have to be anything fancy but of course the better the video quality and sound quality, the more likely you will get buyers. If you have some video editing skills, it can come in handy in terms of offering gig extras. However, all you really need for this gig is a good camera and some basic editing software. The software you need will just have to allow you edit the video so you can remove footage as needed as well as allow you to save the video in common formats such as .AVI or

MPG. Many camcorders come with editing software and even options to directly upload recordings to YouTube and DropBox.

The alternative is to model with a sign and take a picture if you don't feel comfortable speaking into a camera but would still like to be in front of one. You can still use the information in this section but the category would be Advertising > Hold Your Sign. This type of gig is not as popular as doing a video testimonial however.

Do you have to be a model or Brad Pitt to find success doing this? No, in fact, the more average you look, the more likely people will want to do business with you. They want the average Jane or Joe to provide a testimonial for their business as it's more believable. If you can provide some sort of unique personality for them (old business man, excited girl, college guy, etc) and can deliver on camera with confidence and good speaking ability, you will make **a lot** of money doing this.

Another thing, if you have a limited English speaking ability or a foreign accent, it's okay! I have yet to see someone do this. I think there is potential for English testimonials from non-native English speakers.

This is also perhaps the fastest way to get your gig featured and become a Top Rated Seller. Fiverr loves this stuff and it's pretty evident on their website. Don't believe me? Go to the Video & Animation > Testimonials & Reviews by Actors category and check for yourself how many of the sellers in this category are Top Rated Sellers. If you feel like you'd have the knack for this or this motivates you then I suggest you at least try it. Let your personality show and have fun with it. The more fun you have with it the more successful you will be doing it.

**Gig Title:** This will vary. I found the keywords, titles and description you use won't matter so much. Buyers *will* find you. This is a high demand gig and many buyers are always looking for new faces because after a while, the Top Rated Sellers become too well known and using them in a video can be risky as visitors may have seen them in other videos. I know that sounds crazy but I stumbled across a video with a user from Fiverr before!

If you offer some specialty or feature, like a green screen or computer in the background of your video, include this in the title. It will differentiate you from other listings. Include HD in your title if you offer it.

**Category:** "Video & Animation > Testimonials & Reviews by Actors"

**Cover photo:** A 1100x260 photo of yourself doing something fun or exciting. That photo of you in a food fight or on the back of a horse should go here. This is your opportunity to express yourself and your personality.

**Gig Description:** Most of the successful Video Testimonial gigs offer 50 words or 30 seconds for $5. I would recommend the same or offer a little more starting out to get that initial rush of sales and reviews then bring it down to something more reasonable. To make your life easier, state that a script for the video is required. You don't want to be writing your own copy and wasting your time on revisions when the buyer isn't happy with what you said. State that you will take some liberties with the script to make it more believable or natural if required. This is good because a lot of the scripts you receive will be awkward to say and sound robotic or unnatural. State that you will offer 1 revision and only within reason. Revisions are only offered when you make a mistake with the script or video. Believe me, if you don't make this clear you will have people working you as if they paid you hundreds of dollars for your video. I feel like most buyers forget you're only making $4 on the video. If there are types of videos you do not wish to make, state it. If you feel uncomfortable doing testimonials for dating sites or pharmaceuticals then make it clear.

**Gig Gallery:** This should include samples of your work. Whenever you deliver a gig, be sure to include it in your gallery. Fiverr will give you this option when you upload and deliver work to complete an order.

**Gig Video:** Obviously this should be you, in all your glory, in front of the camera looking and sounding confident while having fun. Keep it short and sweet, remember to state your gig is exclusive on Fiverr, and show off some of the features (such as background music and green screen) if you have any.

**Duration:** I recommend 3 days in the beginning then 7-10 days when you start getting 10+ orders a day.

**Tags:** "video testimonial" "spokesperson" "review" "commercial" last keyword could be a feature such as green screen, HD, music, business, etc.If you don't know what else to use, use "spokes person" to cover the other variation of this spelling in searches.

**Instructions to buyers:** "Thank you for your order. Please provide me a little information on your product/service/website, a script up to 50 words, the tone of the video as well as any features you'd like to include that I offer. Remember! I only will do 1 revision within reason. Please no requests after ordering. I only do what I offer in my gig description!"

## IDEAS FOR GIG EXTRAS:

**Express gig extra:** If you are able to complete a video in 24 hours, charge $20. Otherwise, I'd recommend a $5-$10 extra to have the video completed in 2 or 3 days.

**Use green screen, include background music, some other feature etc:** If you can offer the buyer a unique feature for their video such as a green screen, some nice background music, a cool effect or a fancy outfit, include it as a gig extra. Depending on how easy the feature is, charge more or little for it. A fancy outfit I'd charge $5 but a green screen effect I would charge $20.

**Deliver your animation in HD:** This is no additional work for you besides processing the video in a larger format but why not charge more for it? Charge $5.

**Include your logo as a watermark over the video:** If you know how to do it (it's easy, just Google it for the editing software you use) you can charge for it. Charge $5.

## APP /LISTING/BOOK REVIEWS

If you have an iPhone or Android or even an Amazon account, you can cash in. Many developers and business owners are looking to increase their reputation or average rating on review sites such as the Google Play store or other listings websites.

If you have an iPhone and iTunes account you can still write reviews on the Google Play store. There is an Android emulator for the PC called BlueStacks. I recommend checking it out and using that so you can write both Android and Android reviews.

Besides app reviews, many users are looking for reviews for their books or products. Business owners are looking for reviews for their listing on Google, Trip Advisor, Yelp, Yellow Pages and more. If you know how to use proxies and create multiple accounts, you can offer more than 1 review per gig, which can help you get more orders.

Fiverr has also begun cracking down on Kindle book review gigs, so you again might need to get more clever with the title. Business listing reviews and app reviews appear to be safe for now. Again, the risk is very low, the worst that happens is Fiverr simply suspends your gig. It's a slap on the wrist, especially considering how high demand these gigs are.

**Gig Title:** This will vary. I would create a gig for each type of review. "write a detailed verified review of your book" "buy, review and rate your IOS and Android app" "write a review on your Google, Yelp, Yellow Pages listing" "write a detailed product or website review" "write a positive and amazing X review"

**Category:** "Writing & Translation > Reviews"

**Gig Description:** Be sure to include that buyers must include the cost of their apps/books. If their book or app costs up to $4, they must purchase a gig extra or additional gig multiple to cover the cost of you purchasing their product in order to review it.

If you want, you can state that any buyers with paid apps or books must contact you first. I just did it as above where I allowed them to give me money to buy their apps/books.

If it's a review for a listing on a site such as FourSquare or Google, be sure to include you will leave a review for any business listing site, in case you leave some out. You could also create a bullet point list of all the websites you will leave a review for.

Most buyers will request a word count so I suggest offering a 100-300 word review.

**Gig Gallery**: This could include screenshots or samples of your work. The photo you upload as your gig picture could be like above. A picture of yourself with logos of all the products/services you can review.

**Gig Video**: I highly recommend using a video of yourself talking about how you will leave a detailed review for whatever you are offering. Be sure to include logos in your video, it makes a nice eye catching thumbnail. Be sure to include that the gig is exclusive to Fiverr.

A lot of sellers do not have videos for these gigs. This is an opportunity to stand out in this category!

**Duration**: 1day initially then no more than 2-3 days if you receive a lot of orders.

**Tags**: "... review" ... being whatever you're reviewing, so app, book, etc. "Kindle" "iOS" "Apple" "Android" "rating" "iPad" "listing" "business" "testimonial" "Amazon" "verified"

**Instructions to buyers**: "Thank you for your order! Please provide a link to the_ that you need reviewed as well as any information you'd like for me to include in this review"

## IDEAS FOR GIG EXTRAS:

**Express gig extra:** 1 day rush for $5 works best.

**I will buy your app/book for up to ...:** You could also use the gig extras to cover the costs to buy the buyer's app or book that needs reviewing. So a $5 gig extra would cover up to a $4 book/app, a $10 gig extra would cover up to an $8 book/app etc.

**I will vote up every other positive review:** Good for sites like Amazon. Charge $5.

**I will include an additional 2 reviews:** 2 more reviews for the price of one. This is good if you know how to create multiple accounts and use proxies. Charge $5.

### 3D BOOK COVERS

I have a bonus video you can watch where I walk through how you can easily generate a 3D e-book cover (really popular with Kindle authors!) to create a mockup of a book for $5.

## GIGS THAT TAKE TALENT/TIME BUT ARE IN DEMAND

There are gigs that I do know are in high demand and a lot of users come to Fiverr looking for them but I am personally not familiar with them since I've never sold them or tried to. The reason is that these gigs take some sort of specific talent and some more time than the gigs above. If you have the talent for the following gigs, I highly recommend you do them. I can't be as detailed on how to set these gigs up but a good way to start a new gig is to search for the gig you want to create, sort by highest rating, and imitate and copy the gig titles, descriptions and tags the bestselling gigs use.

Remember, a lot of these gigs also allow you to up sell and cross- promote other services or offer expensive gig extras for larger work or tasks.

**Translations:** If you speak, read and write in another

language, this can be a huge asset on a website like Fiverr. A lot of people look for translators for cheap, especially for Spanish or French. The category for this is Writing & Translation > Translation.

**Voiceovers:** After buying those gigs for animated videos someone will have to do the voice over, right? If you have a good microphone to capture audio and can speak well and confidently or even have a great voice, it's in high demand and something worth considering. Do something up to 60 seconds for $5 and be sure to include it in Music & Audio > Narration & Voice-Over.

**WordPress support/installation:** If you go under Programming & Tech > WordPress you will see a plethora of Level 2 Sellers and Top Rated Sellers and lots of high ratings and orders. Users will come to Fiverr looking for someone to install WordPress for them cheap or look through their installation and site to resolve bugs and issues. This is a great gig to offer, especially if you up sell other similar services such as web design or SEO.

**Video editing:** Include the word "professional" in the gig title. This seems to be a pretty popular gig but you might want to have buyers contact you for a quote if their project requires more work than what you offer in your gig description. The category for this gig is Video & Animation > Editing & Post Production.

**Mobile app development, testing, icon design, etc.:** This is huge. At the time of writing this e-book, gigs for app develops has grown to be very popular and highly in-demand. Fiverr's most popular gigs are social marketing and SEO but I see gigs that involve app development or gigs for app developers as the next trend on Fiverr.

If you know Java or have good graphic design skills to design an app icon, I strongly you suggest creating gigs in this market. There is a lot of potential here and I do see growth for it on Fiverr in the near future. So much so, that I'm predicting it might even have its own category or sub- category soon.

**Logo Design:** This is extremely popular on Fiverr. I would recommend offering 3 mockups or so. "I will design 3 professional logos for $5" is a good place to start. Up sell and cross-promote if you are a graphic designer and offer more features to the logos in gig extras to increase the average earnings per order.

# CHAPTER 5:

## ACHIEVING FIVERR SUCCESS

### DEALING WITH FIVERR USERS AND PROFESSIONALISM

Always start your messages or responses to order updates with "Hey!" or "Hi!" and always sign off every message with "Thanks, Name". This is basic stuff but it makes you look like a human being. Also, a lot of sellers on Fiverr are not courteous or professional, so stand out. It's an extra 3 words or so you'll have to type. Just do it.

Remember to be polite but firm. Don't bend to user demands, politely decline demands for things you do not offer.

You may come into users who expect the world for $5. This is very common on Fiverr. You need to just make it clear what you provide for $5 and even call users out who message you with crazy requests.

Be diplomatic though. Don't be aggressive. If a user is not happy always offer a refund. I go into this much more in Chapter 8.

### GETTING YOUR FIRST REVIEW

The most important thing when it comes to making your first sale on Fiverr with a new gig is positive reviews. This is also one of the key things when it comes to being successful on Fiverr. Most users, when searching for a gig, will sort the results by highest rating. Also, the first thing they do when they click on your gig, before even reading the description, is read the reviews. You do it, I do it, we all do it when it comes to anything. Booking a hotel online, buying a book from Amazon, we all like to read the reviews.

HAVING EVEN JUST 1 GLOWING REVIEW ON A NEW GIG WILL GET THE BALL ROLLING AND BRING IN THE SALES WHICH IN TURN WILL GIVE YOU MORE REVIEWS.

One way to do it is to buy a review. There are users who will do it on Fiverr (indirectly) or you could even Google "buy Fiverr reviews" and you may come across some discussion forums. You could also go to a site like freelancer.com and post an ad asking for someone to "try" your Fiverr gig and leave you a positive review for it. You could pay someone as little as $5 for it plus the cost of your gig (another $5). It's an investment, yes, but it will pay for itself once 3 people buy your gig. This is not the way I would recommend however. This costs money and this isn't a way with a lot of integrity.

**GETTING YOUR FIRST ORDERS AND GETTING THE**

## BALL ROLLING

The most difficult thing on Fiverr is maintaining consistent sales.

Getting your first order is not that difficult and if you haven't even had 1 order, this section is for you too. The key thing to do if you're a Fiverr newbie and you just created a bunch of new gigs is to sell yourself short,

over-provide and offer something outrageously more than what someone expects for only $5. Bear with me here, I know it sounds counter-intuitive but I will explain.

If you're selling, for example, a 100 word video testimonial (if this is the average for $5 on Fiverr), consider changing from 100 words to 500 words. Over provide and under value on all your services in the beginning of your Fiverr career. Realize that once you start getting sales you can always change your Gig title, description and everything else so that it is back to a more reasonable work load.

In the beginning it will be too much work for a measly $5. You may even lose money for example by paying an outsourcer for 10,000 Twitter followers for $4 because you are selling that many followers on Fiverr for

$5.

It's okay. The whole point here is to drive a lot of sales

initially, thus more positive reviews, and then bringing that level of effort and quantity down to something more reasonable. When scaling it down, be sure to scale it down slowly. Don't go from offering 10,000 followers to 500 followers the next time. Go from 10,000 to 6,000 to 1,000 over the course of 3 days for example.

## YOU GOT YOUR FIRST ORDER! NOW WHAT?

Congratulations! When you finally get that first order, go ahead and get started on it. When you're ready to deliver the order, it's very simple and straight forward.

Go to the order page and click the big green button "Deliver Order". If your gig requires you to upload something to your buyer, say a video or picture, you can do it in the popup that appears when you click Deliver Order. I will go into more detail in the next chapter on exactly what to say to your buyer when you deliver your order and also my system to make delivering gigs as quick and seamless as possible.

When you start getting about a dozen or so orders a day, it's time to not be so overzealous. Don't respond to every order right away. Process your orders in bulk. I will get into this in the next chapter where I talk about my system. My system keeps you off Fiverr and only on it for the minimal time possible. When you get dozens and dozens of orders and messages a day, you will begin to feel overwhelmed. This is why it's important to not get into the habit of responding to each order right away individually.

## RANKING YOUR GIGS (FIVERR'S ALGORITHM)

Fiverr's changes and updates seem to have been affecting everyone lately. It seems that sellers that have been getting a consistently high number of impressions for their gigs, saw them suddenly drop off. Other people have seen random spikes in their gig impressions.

I'm not an expert on the Fiverr search algorithm. I'm not even sure how it works, nobody does. This is all speculation from me and other Top Rated Sellers that I have spoken with.

Firstly, it seems like everytime there is a Fiverr update, like Fiverr 2.0 and 3.0, Fiverr makes a major change to the search algorithm and it seems to reset everything. Every gigs starts to reindex again from scratch, giving everyone a fair shake on getting the top spots for highly searched keywords.

It seems with Fiverr 3.0, Fiverr plays roulette with the top spots. A few weeks your gig might appear in the top 3 spots for a search term, then for another few weeks it's not there and your impressions drop. I'm unsure whether or not Fiverr does this on purpose to try and give everyone a fair chance of having their gig appear at the top of searches.

So what can you do about it? Unfortunately there isn't much. Fiverr doesn't tell us anything about how the algorithm works nor do a seller's stats reveal what keywords people are finding their gigs through. If it told us that, like Google Analytics, it'd be a lot more obvious what keywords we should focus on. Plus, if everyone knew how the algorithm worked, every seller would try to manipulate it and exploit it. So, it's understandable why this is the way it is.

## But There Is One Thing You Can Do That Helps

One effective way to try to rank your gigs is to simply search on Fiverr what you think buyers would search for to find your gig. Take a look at the top 3 gigs that come up. Look at what their titles are, the keywords they use, common phrasing or word structure they use for their titles and Gig descriptions. Take a look at the gig extras they offer and what tags they use.

I'm not saying completely copy your competitors because that won't work. What you want to do is tweak your gigs and improve upon what your competitors are doing.

Another thing you can do is simply create variations of your gig and test them up against one another. Obviously you need to make them different enough so that Fiverr doesn't shut them down for being duplicate gig.

For example, if one of your gigs is "I will write a 500 word article for you" create a variation that says "I will create a 600 word blog post for you" and change the description slightly as well. Use different keywords, different phrasing.

## OR SIMPLY DON'T RELY ON SEARCH TRAFFIC

If you're frustrated by constantly up and down impressions on your gigs, simply stop relying on search traffic. Instead, focus on getting return customers. Contact buyers a few weeks later and follow up with them, offer them deals if they do business with you again. Or simply provide an excellent product that people will want to come back to you.

## SOME SPECULATION ON WHAT MIGHT BE RANKING FACTORS

So, obviously, gigs can't simply rank on just the keywords alone. There must be other factors that Fiverr looks at when it decides how it ranks your gig in certain searches. Again, this is all speculation, but trying to improve on all of these factors couldn't hurt anyway.

**Reviews:** Having a lot of reviews and positive reviews might tell Fiverr that you are offering a quality gig. This could help bump it up in popular searches so that buyers see the best available first.

**Cancellations:** Having a gig with a low number of cancellations might also be a factor Fiverr's algorithm look at. Having a low cancellation percentage, especially in the past, seems to be important.

**Late Deliveries:** A low number of late deliveries on your gig could tell Fiverr that you're a good seller.

**High Average Selling Price:** If buyers are frequently purchasing your gig extras or purchasing multiples, that could tell Fiverr's algorithm that you are offering a lot of value.

**Average Response Time:** Having a short average response time tells Fiverr you are an active seller. Being an active seller means buyers are responded to faster, meaning they have a better experience on Fiverr overall.

**Seller Level And Gig Video:** Naturally, we all see that Top Rated Sellers have a little more ranking power than a seller with no level. A gig video used to also be a huge factor for ranking in the past, it might still be important to have on all of your gigs.

Overall, there seems to be a theme. If your gig is awesome, you deliver a good product, have good customer service and you're making Fiverr a better place, it only makes sense that Fiverr's algorithm will try to put you in front of more searches. It makes sense for Fiverr to do this. They want to expose the best stuff first so that the people spending money on the site have a great experience, come back and tell their friends about it.

## BUYER REQUESTS SECTION

Under the "Selling" tab, you will see "Buyer Requests". The Buyer Requests page gives Fiverr users a place to request a gig or request a specific type of work. Depending what categories you create your gigs under, you will only see Buyer Requests relevant to your current gigs you have up. So, if you have a lot of gigs under the Graphics & Design category, you will see many requests asking for graphics, logos etc.

Here, you may respond to one request per day. You will see dozens and dozens of requests, if you see one you can do, you can click "Send Offer" and choose from one of your related gigs to send to this buyer. Sometimes though, the gigs it lets you choose from are not actually relevant to the buyer's request but you still want to contact the buyer to let them know you can help them. What do you do? Fiverr does not let you contact the user directly through here and you're only able to send an offer. However, there is a little trick you can do. Copy the user's username and paste it to the end of this link:

http://www.fiverr.com/conversations/

So for example, if their username is bob123, the link would be http://www.fiverr.com/conversations/bob123

To improve your chances even more, besides just sending them a message, you can now send them a custom quote for the job that they're looking for. So under the message box on the conversation page, you will see a link to send this buyer a custom quote:

I wouldn't spend too much time on the Buyer Requests section. This section is mostly hit or miss. Most of the requests ask for A LOT for only $5. They are looking for desperate people. Don't be one of them. In the next chapter I talk about how I incorporate this section into my daily Fiverr routine, but I never spend more than 5 minutes on this section. It will not make or break your success on Fiverr or even help it all that much.

You're much better off going under the "Buying" tab and using this section to make a request. You could always make a gig request like "Promote my Fiverr gig for $5" and see what kind of offers you get and even entertain some of them. From my personal experience, the best offer I got was to promote my gig to all their Twitter followers. I didn't do it, but it's a decent option worth experimenting with if you want!

Lastly, ensure that you are always accepting custom orders. Go to My Gigs and enable the option.

## GETTING REPEAT CUSTOMERS

Now, you've sold quite a few orders and you have many happy customers who left you positive reviews. What now? Try to get repeat business, of course!

We do this by following up with happy customers 1-2 weeks later. In the beginning of your Fiverr career, this is a great way to squeeze out more sales and get more reviews. Later on though, you may be too busy or this may be too much work than it's worth. When you're just starting out or are trying to become a Level 1 or Level 2 seller, this works great.

Create a shortlist of Fiverr users who left you a positive review on one of your gigs. Contact them all in a few days to up to 2 weeks with a message like this:

*"Hey username!*

*Thanks again for buying my GIG NAME HERE gig and leaving me a positive review! It helps me a lot. I wanted to offer you something special since you've enjoyed my gig! If you're interested, I will offer my gig <here you offer a little more than what you offered before for only $5. So, if you gave them 500 Twitter*

*followers, offer them 700. If you gave them a 50 word video testimonial, offer them a 100 word for $5, etc>.*

*I would be more than happy to offer this to you! If you're not interested, it's cool! I was just in a generous mood today* ☺

*Anyway, hope everything is well with you! Take it easy!*

*-Name"*

If you want to grow your sales on Fiverr, and build up your seller profile and name on the website, it's the little things you do in the beginning (or starting now) that will add up for you.

Just like any service business, exceeding your customer expectations can go a really long way. In this case, exceeding Fiverr buyer expectations, and going above and beyond what they expect from a simple gig, can really help grow your sales.

Typically, the average Fiverr seller will get an order, fulfill it, and deliver the minimum work possible to keep the customer happy. This is okay on most occasions, but if you're just starting out or struggling to bust a plateau, every single sale you get should matter much more to you.

If you treat every sale like it's your last, buyers won't have any other choice but to leave you a glowing review, tell their friends and other buyers about you, and come back for more.

By exceeding buyer expectations, especially early on when you're only getting 1 or 2 sales a week if you're lucky, a slow growth can happen when you take a little more time with each gig. It's all about growing your customer base, and getting 5 star reviews on all of your gigs early on.

However, not all 5 star reviews are the same.

Sure, you can do the minimum and get 5 star reviews everytime. But what if I told you that you could do a little more and get tremendously positive reviews that make it a no-brainer for new buyers to purchase your gigs, and a no-brainer for your current buyers to recommend you to other people.

I'm not suggesting you do an outrageous amount of work for a measly $5 either. I don't expect you to over deliver forever and I don't expect you to slave away for buyers who already expect too much.

So how can we over deliver without killing ourselves as sellers?

There are two proven ways to surprise your buyers and exceed their expectations.

## 1. THROW IN A FREE GIFT

When you deliver a gig to your buyers, what do you usually include? What they asked for and maybe, if you care enough, a nice personalized message.

When sellers try to over deliver, they go too overboard. For example, if they create logos, they'll throw in 10 variations instead of 1 to try and impress their buyers.

This is too much work. It's all about the gesture.

If you create and sell logos on Fiverr, throw in a free gift or bonus.

Maybe a PDF or book that can help your buyer. This can be the same free PDF you give to every buyer early on as a free, surprise gift.

What's in this PDF? Whatever your target buyer would find helpful. If people are buying logos, it's likely they have a website or business. Maybe a short PDF on branding or marketing.

If you sell voiceovers, maybe a short PDF on editing or a list of great free editing tools.

It's the little things that go a really long way as a Fiverr seller.

Alternatively, you can throw in a free gig extra. So, when you deliver your gig, surprise them by saying "Hey, I know you didn't order the X gig extra, but I threw it in this time, just for you because I thought your project was cool!"

## 2. THROW IN A "COUPON"

Another great trick to get customers coming back, while

exceeding their expectations, is to throw in a coupon or future freebie.

For example, when you deliver your gig, tell them "Hey, I really enjoyed working on this project! Feel free to order again in the near future, if you do, I'll throw in any $5 gig extra for any of my gigs for free!".

So, unlike the free gift method, this isn't over delivering upfront. This is the promise of over delivering on the next order. This might be better suited for sellers with a large volume of sales that are unable to over deliver on every order.

However, this is not as effective as the first method, free gifts, when it comes to exceeding buyer expectations. While they still might expect it, and they would be more than happy for receiving it, immediately throwing in something for free is your best bet if you're trying to make a lasting impression on buyers.

The best part about it is that you don't have to put in extra work for each buyer. You can create a free gift bundle, almost like a gift bag, to all your first time buyers. People love free stuff and free helpful resources. You can throw in a resource guide, a how-to, a tool list, a checklist. Get creative and make sure the type of people that buy your gigs would find them helpful and useful. Don't just throw in a guide to guitar playing when you're selling logo design gigs. That will look thoughtless and automated.

Also ensure the content is yours. Don't steal, and don't get lazy. It should be your work (which will allow you to come across as an authority and expert) and you should even consider personalizing each gift. Even if it's as simple as naming the file or PDF to the username of the buyer.

Remember, it's not all just about getting the right gigs and selling them.

There are nuances and little things like customer service which can go a long way for you.

## GETTING BUYERS TO REFER OTHER BUYERS TO YOU

Every time you deliver a gig to your buyer, include a delivery message that encourages them to recommend another buyer to you. It should look something like this, in addition to your regular delivery message:

*If you recommend a buyer to me, let them know to tell me that you sent them and you'll both get a free $5 gig extra on the house, just for being awesome!*

So, not only are you encouraging someone new to buy your gig by offering them a free gig extra, you're also giving the buyer that referred someone to you, with a free gig extra.

Now of course, you don't want to give away the farm for just another referral.

What I would do in this case, would be to clearly state that it must be a

$5 gig extra that they choose when claiming their reward for the referral. That way, if you have a $50 gig extra that is a lot of work, you're not giving that away for free.

So, if you're a logo designer, maybe you give the buyer that gave you the referral and the referred buyer the raw, PSD file of the logo for free, instead of charging them $5 for it.

If you're selling voiceovers, give away the $5 gig extra that adds an extra 30 seconds to their recording.

You can't just ask buyers to tell other people about your gigs. That's not good enough. You also can't just have people who are recommended your services buy it based purely on the recommendation. The key here is that you're offering something. It doesn't have to be a free gig extra, this is just what I think is the easiest to do on Fiverr and makes the most sense for most buyers and sellers.

It's a lot more powerful for a buyer to recommend other people by telling them "Hey, check out this guy that creates logos, mention me and he'll give you a free $5 gig extra" than just "Hey, check out this guy that creates logos". See the difference?

## GETTING YOUR GIG FEATURED OR ON THE FRONT PAGE OF FIVERR

Getting your gig on the front page of Fiverr is huge. It's not as hard as you may think and you don't have to be selling a lot or even be a Top Rated Seller to be handpicked by one of Fiverr's staff.

The first thing is your gig and profile must be "Fiverr friendly". Having a Fiverr friendly gig means you can't be selling a gig that's potentially against the terms of service of another website. So, selling YouTube views or backlinks or writing a message on your cleavage will not get you on the front page of Fiverr.

The second thing to consider is you should have a service that's either very unique or bizarre. If you look at some of the gigs on the front page, you will see many of them are pretty unique services or very strange. Also, offering a gig that's relevant to the time of year (e.g. Christmas themed gig, Valentine's Day gig) works very well too. Some examples I've seen:

- I will make a short video of myself dancing in spandex
- I will draw you in a cool cartoon caricature
- I will write you a love poem pretending to be a distant girlfriend
- I will professionally master your song

I'm not suggesting you to do any of these gigs (especially the spandex one). What I'm saying is, if you can offer something unique or has a twist to a very popular/common gig, go for it.

The third thing to consider is you must have a video for your gig. A lot of front page gigs don't have them, yes, but Fiverr loves videos in gigs, especially ones that are well produced, pimp out Fiverr and have good music.

The last thing and probably something you wouldn't believe works, is to just ask. Yup, email Fiverr and ask them if they'd be willing to feature your gig. Don't just email them a one liner "Hey can you put my gig X on your front page?" Email them a short paragraph on how much you like Fiverr and describe your gig in detail and why you think it deserves to be on the front page.

## UPSELLING/CROSS-PROMOTING OTHER GIGS AND SERVICES

Fiverr provides an amazing opportunity for you to offer and up sell other gigs or services to Fiverr users. Let's say you are a graphic designer. You have a gig on Fiverr "I will design your small business logo for $5". You make a decent amount of sales per day, around 10. After Fiverr takes their cut, you're making $40 per day. Decent but not enough to make a living as a graphic designer. However, what Fiverr is essentially doing for you is building up a base of clientele for you to offer more or other services to outside of Fiverr.

If you have a website or portfolio relevant to the services you provide on Fiverr, you could include it in your bio and maybe even have this link in all your gigs under "Instructions to Buyers" and every time you deliver an order. If you're a freelance graphic designer, this is an amazing opportunity to show off your portfolio to people who are looking for graphic design.

However, Fiverr cracks down on this, you might get away with a link in your bio for a short while but you might get it removed. I'm going to provide you a better trick to get people to go to your website where you sell full and more expensive services.

Every time you deliver an order, recommend another relevant gig or service to your buyer in the delivery message. For example, when you deliver your logo, include a message like this:

*"Did you know I do more than just logos? If you're looking for PSD design for your website or are just looking for more affordable and quality design services, check out my portfolio! www.linkhere.com*

*I offer a 10% discount to all Fiverr users! Just include your Fiverr username with your order."*

This is extremely effective at milking your services for more money. You could also do this to cross-promote other gigs or up sell on a gig you offer. For example, if you sell Twitter followers, why not include a link to your Twitter retweet gig when you deliver your order for Twitter followers?

Better yet, if you sell say 1000 Twitter followers for $5, up sell the service. Tell the buyer when you deliver the order that you can offer him or her 10,000 for $40.

Again, get creative or put your own twists to it. These are just examples of the kinds of up sells or cross-promotions you can do through Fiverr. A huge chunk of your income can come thanks to this if you're a freelancer or entrepreneur.

**Here's a great trick to promote your website/portfolio every time you deliver an order**: whenever you deliver an order to your buyer, upload a PDF as a sort of "work performed", detailing everything you did and brand this PDF. Have your colors, logo and website name and include a clickable link. You can easily create this in Word and save it as a PDF. This is an extremely effective way of sending a link to your buyers without actually putting the link in your messages, where Fiverr will ban you if you did that. This is a completely safe way to get clients off of Fiverr.

## WHY YOU DON'T HAVE TO PROMOTE YOUR GIGS OUTSIDE OF FIVERR

I've never promoted my gigs outside of Fiverr, *ever*. You may have purchased this e-book to find out how to promote your gigs outside of Fiverr but it's really a waste of time to do so and pretty futile. Crazy, right? I know this sounds counter-intuitive but bear with me.

First of all, Fiverr gets enough traffic on their website that you just need to know how to get your gigs to appear in searches which is not that hard if you sell what's in demand. If you sell something very unique and that something people are not searching for on Fiverr, you should probably stop selling it or look for ways for Fiverr users to find it (relevant keywords, get it featured, etc).

Secondly, promoting your gigs on social media or anywhere else outside of Fiverr, is promoting to users who may have never heard of or even used Fiverr. Promoting something like a Craigslist ad or something similar is one thing. But promoting a Fiverr gig to a person who doesn't even have a Fiverr account is a waste of time.

You should spend more time experimenting with your gig titles, descriptions and keywords to see what works, what doesn't, what gets you more page views and what gets you more conversions. Fiverr has a huge user base and gets a lot of traffic that you should be focusing on attracting.

Fiverr does enough promotion. Try searching things like "Buy Instagram followers" or "Buy Vine followers" on Google. You will see Fiverr often appears at the very top because Fiverr pays for ads. I've clicked on these ads and saw my own gigs in the search results on Fiverr. Free advertising!

Now granted if you have a large mailing list or Twitter following where people would be interested in the type of gigs you sell, then it probably won't hurt to promote to them. However, there's no point in going out of your way to find users to buy your gigs. Like I said, Fiverr receives enough traffic, especially if you sell something users come to Fiverr looking to buy.

## BUT... THE BEST WAYS TO PROMOTE YOUR FIVERR GIGS ANYWAY

Because I know a lot of you will ask me anyway and will want to, I decided to add this to the book. Here's the best ways to promote your gigs outside of Fiverr.

### 1. Join niche forums

Getting active on forums is a strong strategy to help you drive traffic to your page. However, just as you wouldn't want someone to go onto your website only to leave a link and never return, you need to show respect to those active in the forums. Answer their questions, show your expertise and avoid giving a sales pitch with every post. Be subtle about it such as putting a link in your signature. Be picky about which forums you choose. Keep it to three to four so that you'll be able to be an active member of it.

Ozzieuk, one of the biggest sellers on Fiverr, started out promoting his SEO services on SEO and internet marketing forums.

### 2. Create a website/blog

Building a website or blog around your Fiverr account shows that you're credible. Don't cheap out with a website that looks like it was made in the 90s. You can choose solid templates from Theme Forest for about $20-$50. Since you'll have full control over the site you can promote your Fiverr account right on the front page. The more effort you put into building an audience, the more money that'll flow in.

## 3. Social Media

Whether you promote your gigs to your Facebook fans or your large following on Twitter, social media is a sure way to increase the traffic to your gigs. Since Facebook has been cutting out how many fans see Facebook pages they've liked, creating a Facebook page may not be worthwhile. Twitter has a lot of potential. You can do routine searches to see who's looking for a service like yours. Determine the keywords people use to search for your Fiverr gig and then use those same keywords to determine what Twitter users are searching for. Another great social platform to drive traffic to your Fiverr page is Pinterest. You'll need to post pictures of things that relate to gig such as an infographic, cool product you make, etc.

## 4. YouTube

If you're selling video testimonials or video spokesperson gigs, surely you will want to have a YouTube channel to promote yourself. But you can also drive traffic from YouTube to your gigs if you get creative enough. If you're selling something like SEO for $5, why not upload YouTube videos about how to optimize your site with Google and include a link to your services. Users searching for ways to optimize their search engine results on Google will be likely interested in your affordable services.

## 5. Comment on blogs/articles

A great way to get your Fiverr profile and services out there is to search for relevant niche websites that have a blog and post articles that are relevant to what you are selling on Fiverr. Most blogs allow you to include a link with your post and if the situation allows it, you could even mention in your comment that you provide a relevant service on Fiverr.

## 6. The Fiverr forum and LinkedIn group

Fiverr actually has a forum to promote your gigs. I suggest trying it out if you're new. You'll get a lot of feedback in there from other sellers and it could certainly help you if you're new to it all. Fiverr also has a LinkedIn Group for sellers. Be friendly and introduce yourself as well as ask for some critiques on your gigs. It will allow you to post links to your gigs as well as receive more feedback to help you improve the writing and titles on your gigs!

## 7. Offer to guest post

If you're knowledgeable about a topic that is relevant to what you are selling on Fiverr, offer to write an article for relevant blogs and websites and in turn have them allow you to include a link to your gigs at the end of the article. It's a great way to drive relevant niche traffic to your gigs with very little work.

Remember to think outside the box when it comes to getting traffic from external sources to your gigs. Fiverr does a good job of promoting your gigs for you and eventually, you will find that you will have to do less and less promotion as your gigs become more and more popular. These are great tips for new sellers who want to get their gigs some initial sales and reviews.

## ALWAYS HAVE 20 ACTIVE GIGS

Not only does this give you room to experiment and see what keywords work, what kinds of gigs sell and more, it gives you the best possible chance at making the most money possible. I have provided you with many methods to make money on Fiverr. You must have 20 active gigs. Once you find the 4 or so that are making 80% of your sales, stick with those. You can choose to always have 20 gigs active once you find success, but it isn't necessary. You will find that only 4 or so of your gigs are the ones bringing you the most money.

If you're not level 2, always ensure you have the maximum gigs Fiverr allows for your level for you to experiment.

## MORE THAN 1 FIVERR ACCOUNT, MORE THAN 20 GIGS – THE SECRET SAUCE (PT.2)

At the time of this book being written, I have 3 Fiverr accounts. I recommend anyone who wants to bust their Fiverr plateaus or exploit the traffic Fiverr receives to create more than 1 Fiverr account. You can be safe with 2 Fiverr accounts from the same IP address. You can use a proxy, if you're paranoid like me, to have 3 or more Fiverr accounts.

The main thing however, is you need to have a unique PayPal

account linked with each Fiverr account. **Do not use the same PayPal account with more than 1 Fiverr account**. Maybe that sounds like common sense to some of you but I have read on internet discussion boards, on two separate occasions, somebody's Fiverr account being deleted because they used their PayPal account on more than one Fiverr account.

Make a Gmail account for each PayPal account you need to create. If you only want one additional Fiverr account, you only need another new Gmail account. This Gmail account will only be used for Fiverr, nothing else. I recommend linking this Gmail account or forwarding the email from this Gmail account to your current email address so all the Fiverr notifications to this account will be forwarded to your personal email.

Create a new PayPal account with this new email address. Set it all up, and you're ready to create your new additional Fiverr account. Obviously, keep the name, bio and profile picture different than your main Fiverr account just to be safe.

You can sell the same type of gigs if you want. Just don't use the same images or videos for your gigs. Hire someone, like I suggest in chapter 3, to create fresh videos for your gigs.

**This is how I am able to make $4000 a month consistently on Fiverr**. I, at one point, had 60 active gigs in total. I presently only have 17 total that are active since they are the ones that consistently make sales and sell the most gig extras or multiples. I follow the 80/20 principle. I looked at all 60 of my gigs over a period of a month and figured out which 20% of my gigs make 80% of my money. I then started to suspend or delete gigs one by one, slowly, over time to decrease my workload while still maintaining a ridiculous earnings figure.

Why? If the other 43 gigs I suspended are only bringing in an extra

$500-$1000 total a month, they're not worth keeping. I'd rather make

$4000 a month on only 17 gigs than $5000 a month with 60 gigs. Less is more.

## HOW TO TELL IF A GIG IS DOING WELL OR NOT

The quickest way to see how a gig is performing is to go under Selling > My Gigs. Here you will see all of your active gigs as well as analytics for them. What we care about here is Page Views and Conversion Rate. For a gig to sell well you want between 400-500 page views in the last 30 days (or more) and a conversion rate of at least 10%. An ideal conversion rate is 15%. The best conversion rate for my top performers is 25%. If you can get more than that, you have done a great job.

It's good to keep track of what gig extras are selling and which are not. I like to give gig extras a trial run for about a month and then evaluate whether or not the gig extra is worth keeping. This is important since Fiverr gives you a limited number of Gig Extras per gig depending on your level.

However, it's important to note that, generally speaking, the more expensive a gig extra is, the less frequently it will sell. Obviously, this depends a lot on different factors including offering a gig extra that's undervalued, but a $100 gig extra will sell less frequently than a $5 one.

## ENCOURAGING GIG EXTRA SALES

If you want your buyers to purchase your gig extras along with your gigs, it's good and common practice to offer lots of value in the gig extras. For example, you sell "600 Facebook Likes for $5". A good gig extra would be "extra 2000 Facebook likes for $10". You're offering your buyers value here and rewarding buyers who purchase your gig with a discount in the gig extra. Buyers can only get this gig extra if they purchase your gig, so here you just made $12 profit selling 2600 likes on one sale instead of just $4.

## DON'T SELL YOUR SOUL ON FIVERR

Are you selling your soul on Fiverr? Should you? Maybe this is a ridiculous question to you? Would you be surprised to hear I get this question often or see it discussed often? I hope to clear the Fiverr air about the first two questions and if you don't know what I'm talking about let me start off with that.

There seems to be some controversy on Fiverr lately. There are sellers quitting on Fiverr and not just sellers who couldn't make money. I'm talking Top Rated Sellers, people who earn a lot of money. They're giving up and they're fed up. Why? They feel like they're selling their soul on Fiverr.

Fiverr and its buyers ask for a lot. They want more and more for as little as possible. It's very competitive. A lot of buyers forget that sellers are actually only making $4 per gig, not $5 and that they're already getting a lot as it is for such a bargain of a price. A lot of sellers get frustrated by all the demands and the expectation that many buyers have now and it's only getting worse at an alarming rate.

It's not just about the money either. Yes, slaving your time away for a measly four bucks can start to suck the life out of you, especially when you start getting buyers who demand revisions or are unsatisfied with your work. But there's another way sellers are seen to be "selling their soul" on Fiverr. I'm talking about video testimonial gigs, sign holding gigs and other similar gigs.

You've all seen it and you've seen how popular these gigs are and for good reason. They sell really well. No, they sell like crazy.

Especially video testimonial and video spokesperson gigs. So what's the big deal? The controversy is that you're being paid $4 to give a spiel on a product or service you've never even tried or heard of. You're essentially selling your face and voice on camera to help give somebody's business or product some sort of credibility and social proof it otherwise wouldn't have. I'm not going to go into the ethics of this or anything like that but I will admit that doing this gig after a while must really drain the seller.

Still, there are sellers making a killing on Fiverr doing it.

How do we fix this? How do we stop the soul sucking? There are a few ways:

**Be expensive**: Stop selling yourself short and charge more per gig.

Meaning, instead of writing an entire article for 500 words, charge $5 for every 100 words or even 50 words. Guarantee your buyers that the're going to get quality work and the reason they're paying more is because it will encourage more quality out of you by giving their gig the amount of time and attention it deserves. The competition doesn't care how much you charge and there will always be someone who will be able to do it cheaper than you. That's just how business is. Position yourself as the quality/premium seller. You will still get sales and you'll actually be doing work worthwhile. You will increase your hourly rate like this.

**Be selective**: Don't take on every order you get. It's okay to cancel. If you do video testimonials, list the kinds of work/businesses you will not make videos for and be firm. Sure you will lose a few orders here and there but if you think you're selling your soul, it'll keep you on Fiverr longer.

**Don't do the soul sucking gigs**: They're not for everyone. If you're doing a gig that requires too much work for $4 or a gig that you feel uncomfortable doing, stop doing it. You need to enjoy what you sell on Fiverr on some level. You won't last long and you will lose motivation if it's purely about making those $4.

## BUYER REVIEWS

In Chapter 8 I will be talking about how to avoid negative reviews and how to protect your gigs. However, it's important to note that when you deliver a gig, don't expect a review. You should always ask for a positive review in your message to the buyer whenever you deliver a gig (I go over this in more detail in the next chapter) but don't always expect a review. About 50% of buyers will not leave a review. You may be able to bump this a little by, as I said before, asking for a review but don't expect much of a difference. As long as it's a positive review or no review, you are okay.

Also, a buyer could be waiting to post a review. I've had buyers leave reviews weeks after I delivered an order because they wanted to see how my service played out.

## TIP GIGS

If you are selling video testimonials or holding a sign or other gigs of this nature, I highly recommend you create a gig or gig extra where Fiverr users can tip you. You would be surprised on the generosity of most users. They know $5 is not a lot and most of the time, if they're really pleased with your service, they will leave you a tip. I good gig title would be something like "I will graciously accept your tip for $5". The great thing about this is you can even include gig extras in your tip gig to allow Fiverr buyers to give you even more money. Good titles for the gig extras for example would be:

"I will thank you for a free lunch for $10" "I will be jumping for joy for $20"

"I will be able to get some gas for $40"

Things like this. They can be as cutesy or contain as much of your personality as you like. It will encourage Fiverr users to give more.

## IF THIS THEN THAT...

At the time of the writing of this e-book, IFTTT.com has newly implemented Fiverr into their website. IFTTT.com or If This Then That is a website that allows you to arrange "recipes" on the internet where if one action on the internet happens then something will occur for you. This allows you to automate things on the internet. Some sample recipes to give you an idea of how this all works are "If the forecast says it will rain tomorrow then send me a text message" or "If I like a photo on Instagram then send the photo to my DropBox".

Some sample recipes relevant to Fiverr are "If a buyer buys one of my gigs then add it to an excel file" or "If a buyer posts a positive review then post it to my Twitter".

It's still something new but definitely worth checking out. You may find something really useful here for yourself.

IFTTT's Fiverr integration is still very new and the features are very limited. However, this opens up the possibility and potential to automate more actions on Fiverr, including perhaps one day being able to automatically deliver gigs to buyers. It's still early but maybe this will be possible one day and your Fiverr gigs can truly be on auto-pilot.

# CHAPTER 6:

## MY SYSTEM: 8 HOURS OF WORK A WEEK

### EVERCOPY/MY DELIVERY MESSAGE

You're getting orders consistently now and you've probably begun to develop your own little routine. If you get enough orders per day, you will begin to notice it is much too time consuming to answer or begin each gig as they are ordered. You should not respond to a new order immediately, no matter how tempted you are. You want to batch your work then batch your deliveries. When I deliver an order, to keep things stupidly simple, I always send the exact same message with my delivery no matter which gig it is. Instead of typing out my message when I deliver a gig every single time, I copy and paste it.

EverCopy, for example, holds notes that can easily be copied from your browser.

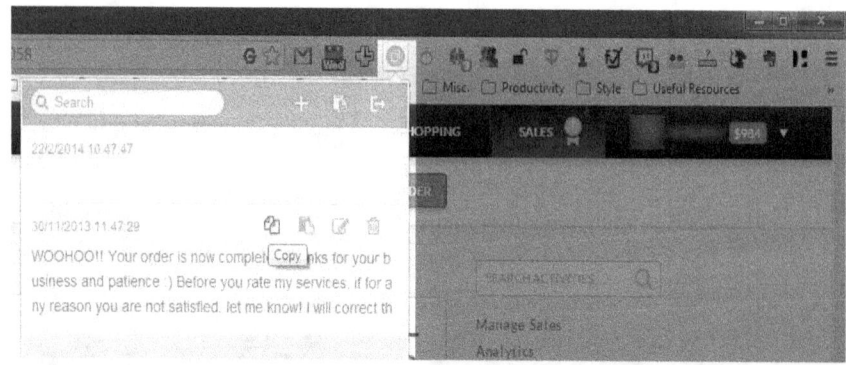

You could easily store your delivery message in a text file and open it up every time on your computer but I like EverCopy as it's a 1 click copy to my clipboard. There are probably similar extensions or add-ons out there for Chrome, Firefox and other browsers. I recommend searching "copy paste notes" if you don't like EverCopy. Here is the exact delivery message I paste into every one of my gigs when I deliver them:

*WOOHOO!!*

*Your order is now complete!*

*Thanks for your business and patience :)*

*Before you rate my services, if for any reason you cannot leave me a FULL five stars, let me know! I will correct the problem or offer a refund.*

*If you're happy with my services, please consider leaving me a full five stars on every category! It helps me a lot!*

Depending on the gig, I may include some kind of disclaimer with this message or my site to up sell a similar service. For example, I have a gig where I do WordPress installation so I link to my web design website to up sell some of my other services. I have a note for each kind of gig so that I can quickly copy and paste these messages when delivering a gig.

## BATCHING

The one thing I must point out is that Fiverr's layout for sellers sucks. It just does. There's no way to leave notes on orders or arrange them or mark which orders you have started, etc. The "To Do" page sucks also. I don't use it and I don't recommend you using it or getting used to using it. It doesn't tell you which orders you've already opened and it doesn't tell you what gig each order is for. All you see is a list of "You need to deliver your order" not knowing which gig it's for.

What I use is the Sales page. Why? Because at least the Sales page will tell you which gigs you've clicked on or read and which ones you haven't read yet. Orders you haven't viewed and haven't clicked on yet will be marked "New" in yellow and orders you've read and have already clicked on will be marked "In Progress" and in blue. You will see how I use this to organize my orders I need to deliver and orders I need to start on in a second.

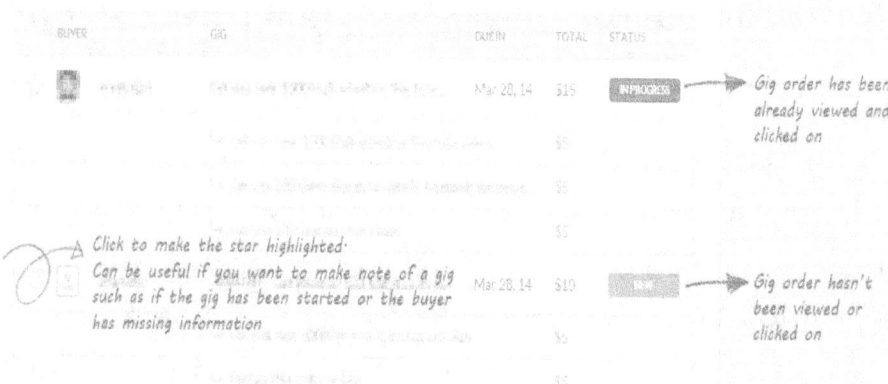

My system is as follows. If I click on an order, I must start it.

Any order I see on the Sales page that says "In Progress" means I've read and opened the order and have started it. If for some reason I can't start the order, for example the buyer didn't provide a link to the site he or she wants backlinks to, I will leave the buyer a message then click the star next on the top-left corner of the page to let me know this gig requires attention on the Sales page.

This will allow you to batch your orders and then batch your deliveries. The first thing you should do when you go to the Sales page is go through the "In Progress" gigs and look at the "In Progress" gigs that are nearing their due date. If you've completed those orders, go ahead and open all of these in a new tab and then deliver all the orders. You can copy and paste your delivery message and hit Deliver if your orders don't require anything else to be included or uploaded. After you deliver the orders that you've completed and were nearing their due dates, go back to the Sales page.

Here, look at all the orders that are "New". Open all of these up in a new tab and process each order one at a time with the information they provide. If a gig can't be started because the buyer has not provided all the information required for example, I will click on the star next to the order and leave a message for the buyer. If I can process the gig, I will leave a message in the order letting the buyer know I have started on the order and I will thank them again for their purchase.

This is a good system when you begin to get 20 or more orders a day.

You can do this routine once a day. Check up on "In Progress" gigs, deliver any that are completed then start all "New" gigs.

## MY DAILY FIVERR ROUTINE

I only check Fiverr once a day to do my daily routine. My daily routine takes no longer than 70 minutes. This daily routine should not eat up more than 8 hours of your week total. It's important to be disciplined and not check Fiverr several times per day. As you get more and more orders you will become overwhelmed so batching all your orders and deliveries is the key to putting your Fiverr earnings on near auto-pilot. Let me break down my routine for you.

1. **Check "order updates":** The first thing I do is I check my email. It's important to enable email notifications so that whenever a buyer updates your order or posts a message in their order, you will know. You could click the speech bubble but you will quickly see how disastrous that is when you have many updates and orders per day. I recommend going to Settings > Account Settings and ensuring you have at least "Order messages" ticked under Email. This way you will get an email whenever a buyer posts a message in their order. The first thing I like to do is check my email and check order messages.

   **The next step of my routine varies on the type of gig I'm selling:** If I outsource my work, I will deliver my gigs before I start new ones. I simply check with my supplier if the work is done, and if it is, I deliver the gig. If I need to do the work myself, I will check for new orders first and complete them before delivering the gigs.

2.  **Deliver gigs:** I follow my system from the previous section "Batching" and open all orders that are nearing their due date and are "In Progress" in new tabs. I then look at each tab, one at a time and make sure the order is complete. Either the supplier I outsourced the work to completed the work that needs to be done or I completed it. It depends on the gig. If it's something that you need to do like videoscribing, do the next step first before this one. This step assumes you already did the work from the previous day. Remember to use something like EverCopy to copy and paste your delivery message into all the gigs that need to be delivered as well as attach any work if required.

3.  **Start new orders:** Here, look at all the "New" orders and open them all up in a new tab. If I sell different kinds of gigs, I like to drag the tabs into some kind of order so that it's something like all the Twitter follower gigs first, then the Facebook like gigs, etc. Obviously, we will start the orders that purchased the "Express" gig extra first before starting others. If I outsource the work, I take all the information from the orders, send it to a supplier and forget about it. If it's work that needs to be done, such as article spinning, I will do it then and there if I have the time or go back to the Sales

page and star the orders to let myself know I have all the information required and I need to complete them. Remember, after opening an order marked "New" Fiverr will automatically mark it "In Progress".

4. **Check inbox for messages:** Answer all questions and inquiries here and remember to follow tips I've provided before and some of the information in Chapter 8. If I don't wish to respond to a message, I mark it "Read" so it won't remain highlighted in my inbox.

5. **Buyer Requests:** If I haven't spent more than an hour on Fiverr, I sometimes like to check the Buyer Requests section. I'll be the first to tell you that a lot of people try to get a lot here for $5. In fact, most of the requests in this section are pretty ridiculous and I'm surprised many of them get a response at all. Still, it is worth checking out as it could potentially lead to a sale you otherwise might not have had.

## FIVERR APP

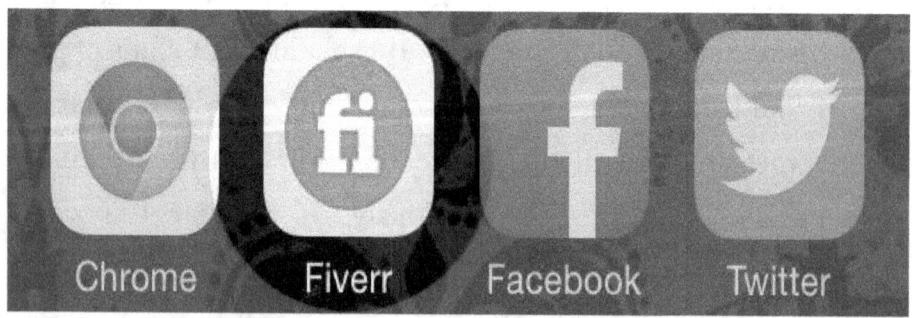

If you have an iPhone or Android (who doesn't?), I highly recommend downloading the Fiverr app, it's free. I wouldn't recommend trying to deliver gigs or anything like that with it but only to use it as a tool for your efficiency on Fiverr. I like to enable the notifications on the app so I can quickly receive notifications of new reviews (positive or negative) and quickly read them, even follow up if I need to. It's also good to respond to inbox messages with. When it comes to checking which orders are due and such, it's not very well laid out and I wouldn't recommend it unless the Fiverr app has been significantly improved by the time you are reading this.

However, at the time of updating this book, Fiverr has announced a new app coming soon for Fiverr sellers, allowing people to deliver gigs simply through their phone, so be on the lookout for that if that app is out by the time you read this.

I also highly recommend going into the App's settings and putting yourself in "Online mode" every time you log into the app. This will allow potential buyers to see that you're online and make you appear more active.

# Chapter 7:

## Road To A Top Rated Seller

I started on Fiverr about a year ago not really knowing what to sell. It wasn't until I found I could outsource SEO work and Social Signals to suppliers for $1 that I knew exactly what I would sell. I always wondered how people did it. I actually started out on Fiverr buying Twitter followers and SEO services before I found sites like SEO Clerks. For the first few months on Fiverr I didn't make any sales. Two things quickly changed it around. The first was I joined a review exchange group I found on the internet. This is how I got my first 1 or 2 reviews for each of my gigs. I then hired someone to make a video for me for my gigs.

At this point I saw a large spike in sales. I went from 0-2 sales a day (if that) to 10-20 sales a day. This is where I saw the true earning potential on Fiverr.

I made a second Fiverr account (to get past the 20 gig limit from my first account) where I only sold SEO gigs. I sold backlinks, link pyramids, directory submissions, and everything else I could get for a dollar on SEO Clerks to resell. I was doing zero work. Every order I got on either account I simply copy and pasted to my supplier on SEO Clerks.

Since I couldn't use myself for the videos on my second account (I already used myself for my first), I got the idea to hire someone to make my gig videos. I joined a "models looking for work" group on Facebook and posted an ad. I got an attractive girl to do all my SEO videos, speaking in the first-person as if she was selling my gigs. This account, with the girl, was outselling my first account with me in my videos.

I quickly earned my level 1 and level 2 on both accounts. The first thing I began to realize though was that on my first account, I would never become a Top Rated Seller. Selling Twitter followers or Facebook likes is frowned upon by Fiverr. There is no Top Rated Seller on Fiverr that sells either.

However, there are Top Rated Sellers that sell SEO services like I was on my second account.

After my second account reached Level 2 status, I did notice a significant increase in orders. I knew this account had a good shot at becoming a Top Rated Seller so about 4 months in, I maintained a zero negative review record. I also tried to always over-deliver when I could and immediately cancel orders for Fiverr users who seemed to be more trouble than they were worth or that asked too many questions. I did this to avoid any negative reviews and it worked.

My average response time to all my orders was 3 hours according to my Fiverr profile. I'm not 100% that this contributes to receiving a Top Rated Seller status but from what I could see, every Top Rated Seller on Fiverr has a very fast response time to all orders and to all messages.

Does this mean I started each order immediately? No, I eventually found my groove and followed my system as mentioned in Chapter 6. Whenever I got messages, I'd respond to them when I could, even on my phone's browser if I had to. This was before Fiverr had an app so it was a little tedious.

Eventually, my account that was selling SEO services was on a roll. I was seeing a consistent number of orders, around 20 per day. 6 months into my Fiverr career, my Fiverr account that I sold SEO services on became a Top Rated Seller.

 EARNED LEVEL ONE  EARNED LEVEL TWO  YOU ARE NOW A TOP RATED SELLER!

I realized that the key was selling Fiverr friendly gigs. You need to mention in your videos that your gigs are exclusive to Fiverr and you need to sell gigs that Fiverr would be comfortable showcasing on their front page. Twitter followers, while they could make you a lot of money on Fiverr, appear questionable to Fiverr. I still highly recommend selling social signals and followers as a lot of people come to Fiverr in search of them, I just recommend you sell them on an alternate account.

Next, you need to make sure you don't let anyone leave any negative reviews and that you always over-deliver when you can.

Always deliver your gigs on time, too.

It appears average response time is a factor too so it's important to be active on Fiverr. I would log into the site once a day when you can, and respond to messages, even if there are no orders to process or gigs to deliver.

At the present time I have 3 Fiverr accounts. Two of the accounts are the ones that I described above and the third is a recent account that does video scribing and article spinning. All my gigs on this account contain videos that are animated using VideoScribe.

# Chapter 8:

## Protecting Yourself As A Now Successful Seller

Now that you are a successful seller on Fiverr, you will need to be vigilant and protect yourself from sabotage/scams from other users. It's not an epidemic on Fiverr or anything, but anyone can become a victim of it, if they're not careful. I will provide some tips of common things to look out for and avoid on Fiverr. I will even tell you what kinds of buyers to avoid. I know that sounds crazy to you right now. "Avoid buyers?? I want every sale I can get!" Trust me, when you're averaging 30-40 sales a day, you will want to weed out the headaches to make your transactions and deliveries more painless and seamless. You will probably ignore most of this advice in the beginning out of greed or inexperience. But, be wise and save yourself a negative review or headache when you can.

### ALWAYS OFFER REFUNDS OR CANCEL ORDERS TO AVOID NEGATIVE REVIEWS

If a buyer requests a cancellation, **just accept the cancellation**. Save yourself headaches, don't even bother asking why, just cancel and move on. Don't be stubborn or too stern. Even if the buyer requests a cancellation after a gig is delivered, accept it. You don't want to risk being left negative feedback on your gig.

It sucks, right? Of course it does! Yes, you may lose a couple bucks, but you will save yourself in the long run. That negative review could have cost you 10 users from purchasing your gig! That's $40 lost because you wanted to make $4. Protect your gig's reviews and never allow anyone to leave a negative review. Make it clear you offer a refund and to contact you in case there is a problem with the gig delivery.

However, there is an exception to this. If someone is coercing you, or threatening you with a negative review in order to force you to do something for free or outside of what you offer: stand your ground. Take a screenshot of the conversation and send it to Fiverr support. They will have your back if you have a case and even **remove any negative reviews this user leaves**.

Which leads me to another thing: cancellations, whether initiated by you or your buyer, are okay. Ideally your **cancellation percentage should be <u>10% or less</u>**. If it is larger than this, there's something wrong. If it's a specific gig that is inflating this number, I suggest suspending or deleting this gig and figuring out why this is happening. However, remember, now on Fiverr, mutual cancellations do not affect your seller rating! So cancel away when you need to!

## WHAT TO DO WHEN YOUR GIGS STOP SELLING

Fiverr constantly changes. Their layout changes, their search algorithm changes. These changes can either make your sales go down or swing up.

If you are part of some of the unfortunate Fiverr sellers who sometimes see their gigs go stale, I have here some tips and ideas to hopefully get your Gigs back to selling!

## Copy Your Competitors

If your best gig stops getting orders all of a sudden, the first thing you should do and the easiest thing you can do, is search on Fiverr for the keyword you want to rank for and look at the top Gigs. For example, if you have a press release writing gig, search "write press release". See what common titles, descriptions and tags the top 3 gigs have and imitate them.

Obviously don't copy their descriptions word for word! See what works for the best gigs, including their images and videos, and use that and apply it to your gigs. This is the easiest way to get your Gigs back on track.

## Experiment With Your Titles / Descriptions / Tags

Now that you have an idea of what titles and descriptions you should make yours look like, experiment with them on your Gigs. Try out a set of titles and descriptions for a few weeks and keep on eye on analytics.

After you see what works and what doesn't, keep playing around with your gig titles, tags and description. Make the title shorter, use a different picture, try a different description and Gig extras.

Getting traffic to your gig is important but you'll also want to experiment with what converts better. Maybe having a better and higher quality Gig video will get you more sales. Maybe something you said in your description is scaring off buyers, bringing down your conversion rate. It's very important to experiment and test different things on your Gigs.

## Create More Gigs

This should be another common sense solution that a lot of sellers miss out on. If you only had a few Fiver Gigs up and they suddenly stopped getting sales, it might be time to create new Gigs! Even if that means creating very similar Gigs, those new Gigs could be the ones that take off.

Remember, Fiverr has a 20 Gig limit and if you're not utilizing that limit to it's full potential, you are actually limiting yourself on Fiverr.

## Scrap Your Gigs And Start Fresh

If nothing else works, it might be time to start fresh on Fiverr. However, if you do this, do not delete your gigs. Instead, suspend them. You don't want to lose the precious reviews you have on those Gigs, if you do have reviews on them already. You can always go back and edit those Gigs or even edit those Gigs with reviews into completely new Gigs!

There are tons of different kinds of Gigs you can sell on Fiverr and start fresh with. If you need some ideas, just check the Conclusion Chapter of this book to have some ideas for Gigs you can start selling right now!

## BEWARE OF: "NEW TO FIVERR/INTERNET/SOCIAL MEDIA" BUYERS

This user will come to you not knowing how to write a review or how to copy and paste his Twitter profile link. They will be a hassle to deal with, and when you deliver the order, they'll ask where it is leaving you flabbergasted.

Look, I sympathize; everyone was a newbie at something at some point.

But trust me, these people will eat your time and they are very hard to please. They expect the world for $5. Try to avoid them when you can. Be polite, a simple "I'm sorry, but I cannot help you" should suffice.

## BEWARE OF: BUYERS WHO ASK TOO MANY QUESTIONS

Whatever you do, don't fall into this user's pit of questions. They will ask you tons and tons of questions. Everything from "what do the Twitter followers look like?" to "Why is the sky blue?". After you go out of your way like a madman/madwoman to answer every single question at lightning fast response time, they will either not buy from you or ask you to modify/redeliver the gig. They are very hard to please and are also huge time eaters. I would also suggest avoiding these kinds of people.

## BEWARE OF: EXTREMELY LARGE ORDERS

So, you get a large order. Somebody just ordered every gig extra you offer on your gig and the maximum amount of multiples. This person just paid you over a hundred bucks for your gig and you're over the moon because it was your largest order ever on Fiverr! Here's the thing, generally, from my personal experience, I found about half of these would wind up in a cancellation or dispute.

I have almost never been able to retain the income from a very large order. What would either happen is the buyer would ask for a cancellation after the order is delivered or the order would be delivered and a week or so later, I get an email from Fiverr telling me this buyer has opened a dispute on PayPal and all the funds have automatically been sent back to the buyer.

The good news is Fiverr always bans/deletes the users who open disputes on PayPal. The bad news is Fiverr never ever fights these and always automatically closes the dispute and give the buyer their money back.

This is troublesome as Fiverr users can potentially leave a negative review on your gig then dispute the transaction on PayPal to get their money back but still have that negative review on your gig. Fortunately, you can contact Fiverr support to remove this negative review if this happens.

## BEWARE OF: "HEY I JUST ORDERED YOUR GIG, HERE'S THE INFO!" MESSAGES

As you get busier on Fiverr and start to receive more and more orders, you will get people trying to take advantage of your busyness in hopes of getting freebies. So, let's say you offer Twitter followers, you may get a direct message in your inbox that reads "Hey, I just ordered your gig, I forgot to include the info, here's the link to my twitter profile: twitter.com/profile Thanks!"

If you look to the top left of the message, Fiverr will say how many sales this user has or had with you. If it's 0, you will not see anything. From a buyer you have done business with you'll see something like "1 Sale" or "3 Sales" which links to all the gigs they purchased from you.

Always double check to see if this person did in fact do business with you, never assume. If they did, always make a point that they should update the order instead of sending you a direct message. If this person is trying to trick you, just report the message, ignore it and delete it. Don't respond, don't waste your time.

## BEWARE OF: RANDOM ATTACHMENTS

I know, this is like advice from 1999. Still, we get so excited with a new sale that we drop our guard with buyers. Never open random attachments in direct messages or orders unless you specifically ask for an attachment from your buyers for your gig. If you're simply asking for a link to the website they want backlinks sent to, then don't be opening attachments if they attach a .zip file instead of providing a simple link. Be polite but firm: "Hey, sorry but I do not open attachments. Please instead paste that information in this order page. Thanks in advance!" A little tip, when you want somebody to do something via email or message, always end in "Thanks in advance", it makes the other party more likely to comply.

## BEWARE OF: PHISHING SITES

As you wheel and deal on Fiverr, you will get links from users depending on what you sell. However, always be careful. If you click a link and you're redirected to a page that looks like Fiverr and asks you to login, it is probably a phishing site. Or, if you get an email from "Fiverr Support" saying your account has been locked and must be unlocked or that they require your password, it is B.S.

Again, I know it sounds like common sense but making you just read that, you are now aware of it and it will always be in the back of your mind. You won't fall into a trap where your information can become compromised.

# CHAPTER 9:

## SUMMARY AND CLOSING THOUGHTS

**KEY POINTS:**

- Always include a video in all of your gigs. Hire someone attractive to do your videos if you can or use yourself.

- Buy reviews or join a review exchange to get the ball rolling on your new gigs.

- Offer more than competitive or similar gigs initially to get your first sales and reviews. Once the orders become overwhelming, edit your gig and offer a similar level of service.

- Always offer a refund and always cancel when needed to prevent a buyer from leaving negative feedback.

- Always have 20 gigs (cut down eventually when you become successful).

- Have more than 1 Fiverr account. At least 2, recommended 3 if you can handle it. This gives you the opportunity to have 60 total active gigs. Work down and suspend gigs as you realize which 20% make you 80% of your money.

- Up sell other services and cross-promote your other gigs and websites in the order messages and in your delivery messages.

- Batch all your orders and tasks on Fiverr.
- Use the same delivery message to keep things quick and simple. Use a browser extension like EverCopy to easily copy your message and then paste it.
- 10% cancellation or less is okay

## MAKING MORE THAN $4000 A MONTH ON FIVERR: IS IT POSSIBLE?

As I started to write this e-book, I began to ponder, is it possible to make more monthly than what I make right now? Most money making books and "gurus" promise millions or hundreds of thousands with their money making methods and I, with Fiverr, only talk about making a measly $4000 a month. Is more than this possible? What kind of work would it involve?

What's the next level on Fiverr? Is there a ceiling to the amount of money possible through this platform?

I will tell you first that most Top Rated Sellers make more than me. I will tell you that many of them don't need or even have more than 1 Fiverr account to achieve this kind of income. But what do they have that I don't? Well, they've been on Fiverr a lot longer, they've been featured or written about, they offer something very unique or different that most people can't offer and, let's face it, they have more sex appeal than me (half of the Top Rated Sellers on Fiverr look like models). But these are excuses. What truly separates them from me is how they sell their gigs.

I will first tell you that I do not charge a lot for most of my gig extras. If you have a gig that encourages people to buy your expensive gig extras, your average price per order will shoot up. How do you do this? You offer something, then you strip away features and services, then you piece meal it to the buyer. Let's say you're an amazing cartoonist who offers a caricature for $5. You don't offer the whole shebang for five bucks. You offer every detail of your drawing separately so that you're not actually offering a caricature for $5 but actually a caricature for $40 or however much. You make the color a gig extra, you make drawing the body a gig extra, you make shading or detail a gig extra, etc. Nobody will want to pay $5 for a simple line drawing. They want the whole thing which could wind up costing however much you charge and the brilliant thing is you can do this with any kind of service on Fiverr. I make my money through volume, of

30-40 orders a day, but you could easily make as much or more with just 5- 10 orders if your money was made through gig extras. You just need to get creative on how you do this. Offer something amazing for $5 and then strip away the services and features. I don't emphasize this in this book because you need to be at least a Level 2 seller for this to work as you can't provide gig extras with a new Fiverr account.

So what if you want to do it my way, with volume, on Fiverr? Is more than $4000 a month possible? Of course! I just need to make another account or maybe 2 and follow this same blueprint I have with all my other accounts. I could easily make $6000, maybe more, if I wanted to. So why don't I? To me, it's putting all of my eggs in one basket. Fiverr is a site I don't own or have any control over. They could easily delete all my gigs and accounts tomorrow if they felt like it. Fiverr is a really nice revenue stream for me but not my only or main one. Having another 2 accounts would require more work and time from me. More work and time that would have to be invested into Fiverr. You could very well do this if you pleased. You could have 4 or 5 Fiverr accounts, each making you enough money that in total you could quit your job and live off of it. It's very tempting too because after you see your first account start to get orders and make money, you'll start thinking about scaling it up. But like I said, relying on Fiverr as your only or main source of income is risky but at the same time you'd be surprised how many people actually do it.

## FIVERR ALTERNATIVES AND CLONES

There are a lot of Fiverr clones or alternatives out there. Just Google "Fiverr alternatives" and you will see marketplaces for $4, $5 and $10 with a similar design to Fiverr. I don't recommend posting your gigs on them or trying to make money on them. None of these sites even come close to the amount of traffic and users Fiverr has. You're better off focusing your time and efforts on Fiverr. Don't try to spread yourself out too thin. Remember focus is important and even if you find success on Fiverr it doesn't mean it's time to find another site like Fiverr to sell your services on. It just means it's time to scale up and earn more on Fiverr.

I have no affiliation with Fiverr, I only tell you to stick to Fiverr because I have tried every known Fiverr clone and they were a waste of time. I saw zero sales from these sites.

## AUTOMATING FIVERR GIG DELIVERIES

There are a lot of sellers on Fiverr who make a decent side income selling products instead of an actual service on Fiverr. I'm talking about things like e-books or software. Instead of trading your time for a measly $4 you can upload a product for every sale you get on Fiverr. Selling products on Fiverr is a lot easier than selling a service and they are surprisingly in-demand if you have a good product because of how inexpensive it is for users on Fiverr. You can't go wrong buying products for $5.

This still takes a few minutes to do, especially when you start to get frequent orders. Wouldn't it be amazing if you could automate this and have software do this for you?

Well you can! Fiverr Automatic Seller is a bot that will login to your Fiverr account and automatically upload your product and deliver gigs for you everytime you get a sale. It's also really easy to use.

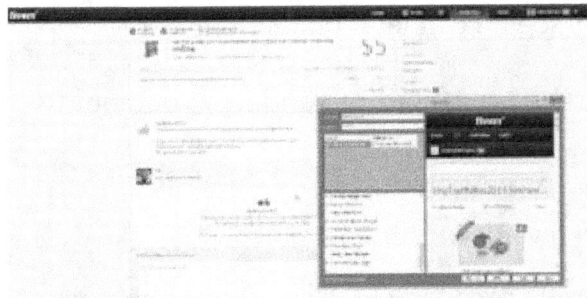

You just boot it up, select the file you want to deliver with each gig you have active and sit back and let the software do the work.

When there is an order, the bot will detect it and quickly deliver the product and gig to the buyer. The bot will also rename the file to personalize it for your buyer. For example, if you're selling diet plans and user "Bob123" buys your diet plan gig, the bot will rename your diet plan file to "Bob123_dietplan", upload the file and deliver it to your buyer.

The software also supports unlimited accounts so you can keep your account that you sell services on separate from your product accounts.

The software also receives updates, so as Fiverr makes physical changes to their system and website you won't have to stress about it. The software will always stay up-to-date with all versions of the website that Fiverr puts out.

The best part about this software is that there is no risk to your account using it. The way it's programmed is not against

Fiverr's TOS so you can let it do its thing care-free.

Wondering what kind of products you could sell on Fiverr with this?

Here's a few ideas:

- Tutorials (videos, PDF's) about any niche. marketing, beauty, health, weight loss, etc
- Graphics package, sales pages, headers, WSO graphics, buttons, banners, etc
- eBooks
- Software (reseller rights, your own products)
- Sites lists (blogs, .edu, .gov, forums, any other script)
- Proxies lists
- PLR Articles
- Leads (list of businesses or merchant of any niche, emails list, etc.)
- Business strategy (online businesses, local businesses, social media, etc.)
- Diets
- Exercise plans
- Ideas for businesses or campaigns of any niche
- Resume templates and cover letter templates
- Powerpoint presentation templates
- Recipes
- And a lot more! You could easily create products in things

you have a lot of knowledge and expertise in and sell it on Fiverr.

If you're interested in using Fiverr as a source of passive income, check out the bot here.

## THANK YOU

Thank you for reading my e-book. I really hope you find success with it or it motivates you to take action on Fiverr. Now it is time to stop reading and just take action. Sometimes we take so much time planning and researching that we become paralyzed by it. We just have to start.

I think Fiverr is a goldmine and an opportunity for most people to make a lot of money online. I wrote this in hopes of helping other people, as I was lucky enough to find success on Fiverr. I worked really hard to breakdown what made me successful on Fiverr and how other people can replicate my success. I must have put over 100 hours into this e-book but I think it was worth it.

I don't think Fiverr Star stops here. I plan on expanding the website with video tutorials and courses as well as maintaining a mailing list and blog for everyone to follow, for free. Fiverr will change and evolve, this I am sure of. Will this e-book be relevant a few years from now? I don't know but I want to be sure that we, as successful sellers, can maintain our success despite any unforeseen changes. Trends will come and go on Fiverr too, so I hope to talk about these kinds of things on my website as well as maintain a good discussion on Fiverr.

Lastly, I love hearing about success stories. If this books helps you I want to know. You can email me at desidofinancial@gmail.com with your story or how my e-book helped you. I love hearing about it! If you have any other feedback or questions, feel free to contact me as well.

On ward to your journey on Fiverr!

**Gianluca S.**

# Chapter: 10

## Conclusion

## Fiverr Gigs You Can Sell Right Now

## Graphic Design

### 1. 3D Book Mockup

There are a lot of authors on Fiverr looking for things like e-book covers and even mockups for their books. You don't have to be a graphic designer or Photoshop whiz to be able to create a great looking 3D book mockup. You can find a lot of templates on Graphic River but you have to be careful with their usage and licenses. There are also free templates on the internet if you search for them.

### 2. T-Shirt Mockup

A lot of people want to see their logos/designs on t-shirts and you can easily whip up a mockup using a template. You can buy a t-shirt mockup template from Graphic River or find a free one on the internet with a Google search. I like Printful's t-shirt mockup generator. It's high quality and it's free.

### 3. Product/Packaging Mockup

Business owners and software developers come to Fiverr looking for mockups for their product and packaging. You can find paid packaging and box mockups on Graphic River but again, there are free alternatives on the internet if you search for them.

### 4. Website Mockup

There are templates on the internet that can mockup a website by displaying it on a laptop or computer screen. This is useful for webdesigners who want to show their clients their design and how it would look on a computer. Graphic River has these kinds of mockups but again, be sure to see licenses regarding usage.

### 5. App Mockup

Many app developers like to include mockups of their apps shown on a tablet or smart phone for the screenshots on their website or on the app's listing itself in the Google Play store or Itunes App store. Graphic River has some excellent mockup templates but again you can find some free if you search for them.

### 6. CD/Album Cover Mockup

Musicians, rappers and DJs are another great demographic of buyers to create gigs for. You can quickly and easily create a 3D mockup of their album cover and cd case using a template from

Graphic River or one you find for free online.

### 7. Logo Design

Logo design is one of the most in-demand gigs on Fiverr, if not the most in- demand right now. You don't have to be a graphic designer or even own any graphic design software to create logos either. Use a free website like LogoYes to create logos for buyers on Fiverr.

### 8. App Icon

App developers that don't have any graphic design skills look to Fiverr to outsource their app icons. There are a lot of ways you can go about creating one, including generators online, but the best way is to find a template and use it.

### 9. FB Timeline Cover Photos

This is a surprisingly in-demand gig and it is very easy to do. There are a lot of free tools you can use to generate a great looking timeline photo. Cover Junction, Timeline Cover Banner, Pic Scatter, and FaceitPages will all do the job.

### 10. Ad Banners

Look for free templates online that are the most common dimensions for ads and use those to create simple ads for your buyers.

### 11. Favicons

You can create one from scratch or ask your buyer to send you a logo/image that you will then convert to a favicon for them with a free converter.

### 12. Word Cloud Image

A new trend for a lot of blogs and websites is to display create Word Clouds for their website for either the most popular/common words used on their website or just words they wish to include in the Word Cloud. There are a lot of free tools online, like this one, that can do it for you.

### 13. Photo Touchup/Red Eye Removal

If you're skilled or experienced with Photoshop, retouching is a highly sought after gig, especially for something such as red eye correction which can easily be corrected in Photoshop or even with a free online tool.

### 14. Simpsons/South Park Character

Another easy to make yet surprisingly popular gig is to take someone's photo and creating a Simpsons or South Park character based on how the buyer looks. Using this Simpsons character creator or this South Park character creator, you can complete an order in 10 minutes.

### 15. Edit Photos/Graphics

Simple graphic design jobs like saving images in different formats, changing the color of objects, and deleting the background from images are all quick jobs you could charge $5 for on Fiverr.

### 16. Turn Photos Into Digital Paintings

Quickly and easily turn someone's photo into a digital painting with either Photoshop (lots of tutorials online) or with a free tool such as this one or this one.

### 17. Turn Image Into ASCII Art

Turn someone's photo to an ASCII art in seconds with text-image.com.

### 18. Turn Image Into Mosaic

Turn someone's photo or art into a mosaic with click7.org.

## WEB DESIGN

### 19. Install WordPress Securely

It's easier than ever to install WordPress, especially one-click installers on most hosts. People will pay for you to do this, and after installing, simply install a security plugin such a WordFence to keep things secure.

### 20. Install WordPress Theme Like Demo

A lot of people pay for premium WordPress templates but they're disappointed to find that it looks nothing like the demo after installing it. These people usually don't realize that most premium themes come with a demo.xml that you have to import using the tool WordPress importer. If you have any experience with this, this is a great and easy gig.

### 21. WordPress Site Transfers

Transfer someone's entire WordPress installation quickly and easily with WP clone. Simply install Wordpress on the new host and install the plugin WP Clone on both installations and clone the original install with the plugin then copy and paste the link into the plugin in the new install. Easy!

# WRITING

### 22. Write/Spin Articles

This is very much in-demand. You can choose to either write the articles from scratch (recommend 100 words per $5) or spin them with WordAi (recommend 500 words per $5). Spinning essentially involves finding an articles from a site like EzineArticles.com related to the niche your buyer wants, then using a spinner or rewriter like WordAi to rewrite the article for you so it passes all plagiarism checkers and duplicate content checkers.

### 23. Articles

If you have the patience to proofread and edit people's work, you can use advanced editing software like Grammarly to edit

1000 words in 10 minutes.

### 24. Book Reviews

Kindle book reviews on Fiverr are really big right now. Be sure to offer a verified review (a review where you actually purchase their book and then review it) and in your gig extras, allow buyers to cover the cost of their book if it's not free.

### 25. App Reviews

App reviews are big on Fiverr, especially for the Android. If you have an iPhone but not an Android device, I would recommend downloading the Android emulator BlueStacks to leave Android app reviews. Remember to include gig extras or encourage multiples to cover the cost of paid apps.

### 26. Listing/Directory Reviews

A lot of businesses have listings on sites like TripAdvisor, Google Places, and FourSquare with no reviews and often times to come to Fiverr looking for someone to leave a review. This is an easy copy and paste gig.

### 27. Press Release Writing/Press Release Submission

Google "Press release template" and use that for this kind of gig. You could also submit the buyer's press release as a gig extra or a separate gig altogether.

### 28. Write Sales Copy/Headlines/Taglines

If you're great at writing sales copy (or even decent at it) this is great, short work.

### 29. Comments On Blogs/Videos/Social Media

Leave comments on people's blogs, YouTube videos or even Instagram photos. Works better if you use multiple accounts and use proxies. For cheap proxies, I like to use BuyProxies.org.

### 30. Indiegogo Campaign

Contribute $1 to Fiverr user's Indiegogo campaigns, share campaign on Facebook and leave a comment for $5 on Fiverr.

### 31. Transcribe Audio/Video

Transcribe 30 seconds of audio for $5. This is a really great gig that can make you a nice hourly rate, especially if you're a good typer.

### 32. Write "About Us" Page

There are a lot of templates you if you search on Google for "About us templates" that you can use to write up great About Us pages for company websites that require it.

### 33. Write "Terms And Conditions" and "Privacy Policy"

Search for Terms and Conditions or Privacy Policies "generator" or "template" to quickly whip up these highly sought after pages for companies and web designers.

### 34. Write Resume Or Cover Letter

Ask your buyer what kind of job they are applying for and ask for their work experience and education and insert that into a resume or cover letter template for the kind of job or industry they're applying for.

### 35. Critique Resume

You don't have to be a job expert or a recruiter, you can quickly critique a 1 or 2 page resume for $5.

### 36. Translation Services

If you are a bi-lingual this is a great in-demand gig. You could even use a free translator and correct the translation so that it is correct. I would recommend 50 words for $5.

### 37. Article Submission

You can manually submit articles as either a gig extra or separate gig for your buyers. Here's a good list of high PR free article submission sites.

## SEO (SEARCH ENGINE OPTIMIZATION)

### 38. Keyword Analysis

Use a keyword analysis tool like Long Tail Pro to create excel reports for buyers showing keyword competition. You can also use Google's Keyword Planner tool.

### 39. Domain Research

Create a gig where you will do domain research for a company and create a report showing which domains are available for their brand/niche that would work best. I like to use Who.Is.

### 40. Niche Research

Perform niche research or supply buyers with a niche that has a good average monthly search on Google and a high CPM for advertisers, meaning it's a great niche to build a website for and place Adsense ads on. Long Tail Pro is a great tool for this.

### 41. Backlinks

Find backlink packages for $1 on SEO Clerks and resell them on Fiverr for $5.

### 42. Send Traffic To Website

Find traffic services for $1 on SEO Clerks and resell them on Fiverr for $5.

### 43. Submit Businesses To Listings

A lot of small and local businesses don't have listings on websites like Yellow Pages and Google Places. Create them for them for $5.

## SOCIAL MEDIA

### 44. Tweet Messages To Followers

If you have a lot of Twitter followers or create an account and buy a lot of Twitter followers for it, you can sell Twitter messages/ads to your followers for $5.

### 45. Social Signals

Buy social signals to a website such as Facebook shares and Google pluses from SEO Clerks and resell them on Fiverr for $5.

### 46. Twitter Followers

Twitter followers are highly in-demand. There are a lot of $1 gigs on SEO Clerks that you can resell for $5 on Fiverr.

### 47. Facebook Likes

Resell Facebook page and post likes on Fiverr from SEO Clerks.

### 48. YouTube Views/Likes/Subs

SEO Clerks is a great place to resell YouTube services from. YouTube views are highly in-demand, especially high retention ones.

### 49. Vine Followers/Revines

Vine services are still new and not highly in-demand as other social media sites, but as Vine grows, so will the demand for these gigs. SEO Clerks has a few $1 gigs to resell.

### 50. Instagram Likes/Followers

Instagram is very much in-demand, especially Instagram likes. Resell $1 SEO Clerks Instagram gigs for $5 on Fiverr.

### 51. Pinterest Followers/Repins

Again, SEO Clerks is a great place to resell from on Fiverr.

### 52. Create Facebook Fanpage/Page For Business

You'd be surprised how many business owners don't know how to even create a Facebook page for their own business. This is a great easy business.

### 53. Setup Social Media, Create YouTube Channel

Better yet, you can have a package where you create pages on all major media services for the buyer's small business on sites like YouTube and Twitter either as a gig extra or separate gig.

### 54. Manage Social Media

Create a gig where you will manage a company's website for a day.

### 55. Share Links/Promos To Twitter/Facebook Followers/All Social Media

Share a link to a company website to all your Facebook friends and all your social media profiles.

### 56. Create And Sell Accounts

You can create accounts for social media websites and sell them on Fiverr. You may need to **use proxies** and create email addresses for each account. You may need to phone verify accounts as well.

VIDEO

### 57. Video Testimonials/Spokesperson/Review

This is very much in-demand and very easy to do. I highly recommend this gig for newbies on Fiverr to start making some money.

### 58. Product Testimonials

Ask for your buyer to mail you a physical product, or record yourself using a virtual one, such as an app, website or game. The idea is to record yourself using the product while providing a testimonial.

### 59. 5-Minute Video Critiques

Instead of writing a critique for something like a website, product or app, why not record yourself offering one? It's much more personalized and it is unique.

### 60. Whiteboard Animations

This is very easy to do and very much in-demand. Go to Sparkol, sign up for a trial and learn the software in only minutes. It's very easy to use and great for creating brilliant animations. I would recommend $5 for 10 seconds of animation.

### 61. Edit Video/Add Music/Graphics

If you have Windows Movie Maker, you could do easy video edits for $5 such as adding music to videos, adding a watermark, etc. You could also use premium software for more options such as Camtasia.

### 62. Convert Audio/Video Files To Other Formats

There are a lot of free converters online but you'd be surprised how many people pay for a service like this. You can convert .AVI to .MP3, or even a YouTube video into an MP3.

## CREATIVE

### 63. Voiceovers

You don't need to be a professional to do this. You could offer 30 seconds of a voiceover for $5.

### 64. Use Pets For Videos/Pictures

If you have a pet, you can use them in creative ways for things like signs, videos, photos, etc. and buyers and Fiverr love stuff like this.

### 65. Take Picture Holding Sign/Message/Logo

This is not as in-demand as video testimonials, but it is still a gig worth trying out if you do video testimonials as well.

### 66. Logo Advertising On Body/Hand/Car/Creative Way

Fiverr loves this stuff and there is a demand for it if you are creative enough.

There are a lot of successful sellers that offer something like this. Basically you can either paint the logo onto yourself, draw it on yourself, digitally put it on yourself or put the buyers logo on other things such as a car or wall.

### 67. Spell Out Name/Logo In Rice/Alphabet Soup/Other

This is an easy gig and Fiverr loves gigs like this and they often feature them. It just requires for you to spell out the buyer's name or logo in a creative way and taking a photo of it. For example, spelling out the buyer's name or logo in rice.

### 68. Sing Happy Birthday

You definitely don't have to be a good singer to offer this. You could have a terrible singing voice, it might even help you sell more. If you get creative with it and wear a costume on video, you will have more success.

### 69. Help Brainstorm Company Names/Slogans

If you consider yourself a creative person, many people come to Fiverr looking for creative help. You could offer 20 company names or slogans for $5. The potential for different kinds of gig extras are limitless here as well.

## Virtual Assistant

### 70. Give Advice

What do you do for a living or have a passion in? You don't necessarily have to be an expert in anything to charge people $5 for advice. Are you good with cars? You could give people car advice. Are you good at dating or relationships? You can offer people relationship or online dating advice.

### 71. Do Research

There are many users who come on Fiverr looking to outsource research work before writing a book or putting together a project. If you're really good at using Google, then you could easily do this. You can claim $5 for 30 minutes of research, but it won't have to take you that long to research a topic.

### 72. Research Amazon Keywords/Niches For Writers On Kindle

There is software that will allow you to find what keywords and niches are in- demand. A lot of Kindle authors, many of whom use Fiverr, would kill for this kind of information. Kindle Samurai is amazing for this. It allows you to easily research a niche or keyword for sellers then export it to an Excel file to upload it to your buyer. 5 minutes of work for $4? I'll take it!

### 73. Teach Lessons/Language

If you are bilingual or know other languages besides English, you could offer short lessons on Fiverr for $5 over Skype. This also has the potential to allow for some nice expensive gig extras.

### 74. Test/Do QA For Apps/Software

A lot of developers need users to test their apps and software to find bugs and provide feedback. So much so, that they are willing to pay for it.

### 75. Virtual/Remote Computer Repair/Cleaning Service

You can use software like TeamViewer or LogMeIn to remotely access a buyer's computer and quickly install software like CCleaner and do some registry cleaning. If they're having errors, and you are good at diagnosing and solving problems (a quick Google search solves most PC errors) this would be a good gig for you that you can charge a lot for in gig extras.

### 76. Virtual/Remote Virus/Malware Removal

This is the same idea, using a remote access software like TeamViewer or LogMeIn and instead, repairing a buyer's computer from viruses and malware using software like MalwareBytes. Again, nothing a quick Google search can't fix yet most people are willing to pay for it.

### 77. Post Ads To Craigslist/Kijiji

Yup, people pay for this and it's more in-demand than you might think. A lot of business owners want users to post Craigslist ads across many different locations, you could do this yourself easily for $5.

### 78. Submit Free Ebooks Promo To Websites

A lot of Kindle authors will put their books free for a limited time to drive traffic and reviews to their e-book. Often, they'll submit this promotion to many of the free e- book websites out there. Because this can become a time consuming task, you can offer to do this for the author, here's a list of sites to submit to.

## DIGITAL PRODUCTS/DOWNLOAD

In this section, I'm going to share in-demand downloadable products. Now, when selling these, you could manually deliver each order by uploading the product to the buyer and completing the order. However, this entire process can be automated so you'll virtually never have to log into Fiverr again.

There is software called Fiverr Automatic Seller that will automate your deliveries. Every time a Fiverr user purchases one of your digital products, Fiverr Automatic Seller will upload the file to the buyer and complete the order. Check it out.

### 79. Graphics Package

If you are a graphic designer you can put together a package of templates or logos that buyers can get for $5. You could also scour the internet for private label rights graphics and resell them on Fiverr.

### 80. Software

Search for PLR software on the internet or sell your own.

### 81. Proxies Lists

There are tons of free proxies on the internet that you could sell on Fiverr for $5. Use a tool like a proxy scraper to gather proxies into a text file and sell that to users.

### 82. PLR Articles

Download or buy PLR articles and resell them on Fiverr. You will need to sell them in large quantities per order for buyers to want to buy them.

### 83. PLR Books

This is the same idea, download or buy PLR books and sell them. You can sell these individually however and they don't need to be bundled.

### 84. Write Your Own Books

You've probably never thought about using Fiverr to sell your book, right? While Kindle is a great platform, you could sell small report books in PDF format instead of uploading it to Kindle or another platform.

### 85. Exercise Plans

If you are into fitness, this is a great way to make money on Fiverr. You could also research exercise plans for say people who want to put on muscle or lose weight, create an exercise plan that is detailed and sell that on Fiverr.

### 86. Diets

There are many ways to create a meal plan online. I like

Swole.me. Ask buyers for the desired caloric intake, their number of meals, what kind of foods they prefer and create a meal plan for them on Swole.me and put it into a document and upload it to them.

### 87. Recipes

There are a lot of PLR recipes out there but you could also share your own or use ones you find on the internet. Recipes themselves are free from copyright, so you don't have to worry about doing anything sketchy.

### 88. Powerpoint Templates

If you're good with Powerpoint, this sells very well as it's cheaper to buy Powerpoint templates on Fiverr than anywhere else.

### 89. Repair Guides/Manuals

You can find information on how to repair and fix commonly damaged items like an iPhone or PS3 and sell that information on Fiverr for $5.

### 90. Ideas For Businesses/Campaigns For Specific Niches

You can have stock marketing plans and business plans for specific niches or niches you are interested in and sell that on Fiverr.

### 91. Resume/Cover Letter Templates

Very much in-demand, a lot of users come on Fiverr are looking for help to find work or make money. You can either create your own resume or cover letter templates or find some that you are able to resell on Fiverr.

### 92. Leads

Email lists are very popular on Fiverr, if you have your own or find ones to resell, this is a great way to make money on Fiverr as the email lists on Fiverr are cheaper than what you'd find elsewhere.

### 93. Business Strategy

You can have stock marketing plans and business plans for specific niches or niches you are interested in and sell that on Fiverr.

### 94. Site Lists

Create a list of websites/resources for specific niches and sell that on Fiverr. For example, 100 tools for your business' social media or 100 websites for entrepreneurs. Many buyers will be glad to pay for a useful like that.

### 95. Tutorials

Write-up a tutorial, such as how to create a WordPress website or how to start publishing on Kindle and sell it on Fiverr. Any short tutorial, as long as it's informative and teaches something can be sold on Fiverr, especially if the right information is hard to find on the internet.

# Misc

### 96. Critique Websites

There are a lot of web developers and business owners on Fiverr, so it would be a good to offer a website critique. You can critique the website through the eyes of an average visitor and offer suggestions and corrections to the design and function of the website.

### 97. Facebook Wall Posts / Relationship Statuses

This is going to be a weird one, but it actually sells well. If you create a fake Facebook profile of an attractive woman, Fiverr users will pay you to be in a relationship with them for 2 weeks or to write things on their wall. I know, it may sound crazy but this is a super easy gig that actually works really well.

### 98. Give DropBox Space Using Buyer's Referral Links

Everyone by now uses DropBox but not many are willing to pay for it to get increased space. DropBox increases your free storage space whenever you refer someone to the service. If you're good with VPNs or Proxies, you can sell increases space on DropBox by allowing the buyer's to send you their referral links to increase their storage space.

### 99. Send Postcards / Create Postcards

If you live in somewhere outside of the US, this gig actually has a lot of potential. It's a new trend on Fiverr and it sells well. Offer to send someone a postcard from your location/country and have them pay for shipping when you create the gig. You can also offer to create a postcard and send it to them as well.

### 100.    Create/Convert To PDF

Offer to convert Fiverr users' documents, powerpoint presentations and excel files into PDF. You don't need to be skilled to do it either, there are a lot of free tools online that can get the job done like this one.